FRANCIS FRITH'S

CAMBERLEY - A HIST
CELEBRATION

GW00728102

THE FRANCIS FRITH COLLECTION

www.francisfrith.com

CAMBERLEY

A HISTORY AND CELEBRATION
OF THE TOWN

HAZELLE JACKSON

Produced by The Francis Frith Collection

www.francisfrith.com

First published in the United Kingdom in 2004 by
The Francis Frith Collection®

Hardback Edition 2004 ISBN 1-90493-814-0
Paperback Edition 2011 ISBN 978-1-84589-618-8

British Library Cataloguing in Publication Data

Camberley - A History and Celebration of the Town
Hazelle Jackson

The Francis Frith Collection®
Oakley Business Park, Wylye Road,
Dinton, Wiltshire SP3 5EU
Tel: +44 (0) 1722 716 376
Email: info@francisfrith.co.uk
www.francisfrith.com

Printed and bound in Great Britain
Contains material sourced from responsibly managed forests

Front Cover: **CAMBERLEY, HIGH STREET 1925** 78125t

Additional photographs by Hazelle Jackson.
Domesday extract used in timeline by kind permission of
Alecto Historical Editions, www.domesdaybook.org.
Aerial photographs reproduced under licence from
Simmons Aerofilms Limited.
Historical Ordnance Survey maps reproduced under licence from
Homecheck.co.uk

*The colour-tinting in this book is for illustrative purposes only,
and is not intended to be historically accurate*

Contents

FRIMLEY ROAD 1931 83848p

Historical Timeline for Camberley

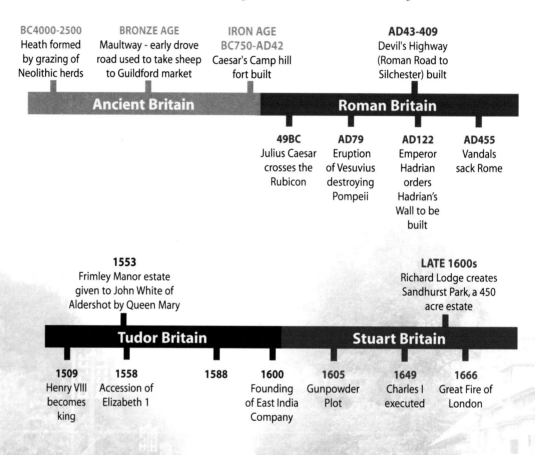

BC4000-2500
Heath formed by grazing of Neolithic herds

BRONZE AGE
Maultway - early drove road used to take sheep to Guildford market

IRON AGE BC750-AD42
Caesar's Camp hill fort built

AD43-409
Devil's Highway (Roman Road to Silchester) built

Ancient Britain

Roman Britain

49BC
Julius Caesar crosses the Rubicon

AD79
Eruption of Vesuvius destroying Pompeii

AD122
Emperor Hadrian orders Hadrian's Wall to be built

AD455
Vandals sack Rome

1553
Frimley Manor estate given to John White of Aldershot by Queen Mary

LATE 1600s
Richard Lodge creates Sandhurst Park, a 450 acre estate

Tudor Britain

Stuart Britain

1509
Henry VIII becomes king

1558
Accession of Elizabeth 1

1588

1600
Founding of East India Company

1605
Gunpowder Plot

1649
Charles I executed

1666
Great Fire of London

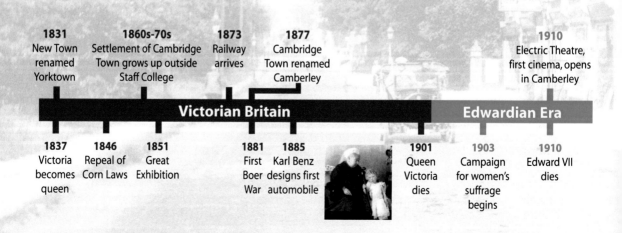

1831
New Town renamed Yorktown

1860s-70s
Settlement of Cambridge Town grows up outside Staff College

1873
Railway arrives

1877
Cambridge Town renamed Camberley

1910
Electric Theatre, first cinema, opens in Camberley

Victorian Britain

Edwardian Era

1837
Victoria becomes queen

1846
Repeal of Corn Laws

1851
Great Exhibition

1881
First Boer War

1885
Karl Benz designs first automobile

1901
Queen Victoria dies

1903
Campaign for women's suffrage begins

1910
Edward VII dies

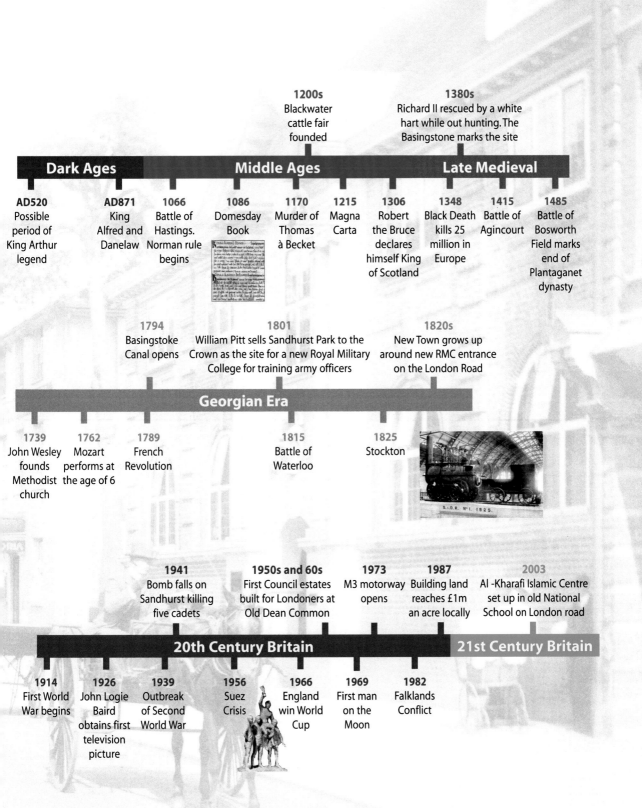

1200s
Blackwater cattle fair founded

1380s
Richard II rescued by a white hart while out hunting. The Basingstone marks the site

Dark Ages | Middle Ages | Late Medieval

AD520
Possible period of King Arthur legend

AD871
King Alfred and Danelaw

1066
Battle of Hastings. Norman rule begins

1086
Domesday Book

1170
Murder of Thomas à Becket

1215
Magna Carta

1306
Robert the Bruce declares himself King of Scotland

1348
Black Death kills 25 million in Europe

1415
Battle of Agincourt

1485
Battle of Bosworth Field marks end of Plantaganet dynasty

1794
Basingstoke Canal opens

1801
William Pitt sells Sandhurst Park to the Crown as the site for a new Royal Military College for training army officers

1820s
New Town grows up around new RMC entrance on the London Road

Georgian Era

1739
John Wesley founds Methodist church

1762
Mozart performs at the age of 6

1789
French Revolution

1815
Battle of Waterloo

1825
Stockton

1941
Bomb falls on Sandhurst killing five cadets

1950s and 60s
First Council estates built for Londoners at Old Dean Common

1973
M3 motorway opens

1987
Building land reaches £1m an acre locally

2003
Al -Kharafi Islamic Centre set up in old National School on London road

20th Century Britain | 21st Century Britain

1914
First World War begins

1926
John Logie Baird obtains first television picture

1939
Outbreak of Second World War

1956
Suez Crisis

1966
England win World Cup

1969
First man on the Moon

1982
Falklands Conflict

CHAPTER ONE

A Blasted Heath

"Much of it is sandy desert where winds raise the sands … The ground is otherwise so poor and barren, that the product of it feeds no creatures but some very poor sheep and but few of these, nor are there any villages worth remembering and but few houses or people for many miles far and wide. This desert lies extended so much that some say there is not less than a hundred thousand acres of this barren land… reaching out every way in the three counties of Surrey, Hampshire and Berkshire."

Daniel Defoe 1724.

THE DEVIL'S HIGHWAY 2004 C12704k (Hazelle Jackson)

UNTIL THE early 19th century the modern town of Camberley did not exist. In its place lay the sprawling wastes of Bagshot Heath - a vast moorland of scrub, gorse and stunted stands of pine trees, spreading over the borders of Surrey, Hampshire and Berkshire. To the north lay the Royal Forest of Windsor; to the south and west the peat moors of Frimley Heath and the valley of the Blackwater river where isolated farming communities like Yateley, Sandhurst, Hawley and Frimley eked out a meagre living. This was bandit country, notorious as the haunt of highwaymen and thieves. Early travellers like Defoe sought to pass through the inhospitable terrain as quickly as possible.

The heath here is formed on the light sandy soil which overlays the clays of the London basin, created when the last Ice Age retreated around 6000 BC. As the sea level around the British coast rose, swelled by the melting ice water, Britain was cut off from Continental Europe. After the last Ice Age, the land left behind by the departing ice became first tundra grassland and then vast oak forests.

Then Neolithic man arrived with his cattle and cleared the trees to graze and corral his cattle. This ground clearance upset the delicate balance of the land and caused the minerals and nutrients to leach out of the unstable soil creating heath as the acid soil was invaded by scrub, gorse, heather, bracken and weed trees.

For centuries local communities grazed their cattle and deer, bred and caught rabbits and collected turf for fuel on the common land around their homes. This constant cropping of the vegetation ensured that the land stayed as heath for centuries. The pinewoods, which characterise much of the area today, were only planted in the early 19th century when the land was enclosed.

Contact with the outside world came slowly for Neolithic man but in the early Bronze Age, from 2,300 BC to 1,200 BC, the inhabitants of Britain first started to work in copper and bronze and trade began to develop with Europe. The prospect of gold, silver and tin lured the Romans to Britain in AD43 and, after subduing the local population, they began to exploit the country's mineral wealth and built roads to move troops, supplies and manufactured goods, to and from the channel ports. A major Roman road, today known as the Devil's Highway, can be traced in the woods here.

Near the Devil's Highway is a large Iron Age hill fort, known since the 18th century as Caesar's Camp. In fact the camp dates from between 200BC and AD40 and was probably later adopted by the Romans as a defensive position near the highway. Early maps describe this area as a Romano-British settlement and archaeologists have found

TREES ON THE HEATH 2004 C12703k (Hazelle Jackson)

traces of a Roman settlement at Wickham Bushes which may possibly have been a manufacturing base for metal smelting. Wickham Bushes derives its Saxon name from the Latin word Vicus meaning 'settlement' or 'small town'.

The Devil's Highway was not the only route through Windsor Forest. A much older route here is the ancient Maultway. This is likely to have been an old drove road used to herd sheep south from the Berkshire Downs over Surrey Hill and Curley Hill and the Chobham Ridges to Pirbright and Guildford, a centre of the medieval wool trade. (The name Mault may be derived from Mollt, the Celtic word for sheep). From the Middle Ages onwards some of the sheep were turned off near where the Jolly Farmer roundabout is today and driven west to the great November sheep fair at Blackwater on the border of Hampshire and Surrey near modern Camberley.

According to Old Moore's Almanac the Blackwater Fair was, for centuries, the largest cattle fair in the South of England. Cows, horses, pigs and sheep were taken there to be sold, even ponies from the New Forest and cattle from the West Country and Wales. The fair was a byword for heavy drinking, honest and dishonest trading and licentious behaviour. There are reports of prize fights and later of swings and sideshows.

After the Romans left the British Isles around AD410, their road system decayed and fell into disuse. During the Dark Ages the Royal Forest of Windsor Forest to the north covered a large area adjoining Bagshot Heath. A forest at this time was a large unenclosed area of land, which could include woodland, heath, scrub and even farmland.

The primary function of a Royal Forest was for rearing and hunting the King's deer; stags in particular were regarded as a royal animal and reserved for the monarch to hunt. Royal Forests were also a valuable resource to medieval monarchs; besides venison they ensured a ready supply of timber, small game, wild plants and fruits. Royal Forests belonged to the king and were assigned a protected legal status, 'afforested', which made them subject to special laws to preserve and protect the King's deer.

When William the Conqueror came to power in 1066 he increased the number of Royal Forests and enforced a strict French version of Forest Law to preserve the venison and vert (green undergrowth for feeding the venison). Royal Foresters enforced these laws and punishment was severe. Taking and killing the King's deer in a Royal Forest was

ARTIST'S IMPRESSION OF A NORMAN SHIP F6019

still preserved in some ancient forest areas today, like the New Forest in Hampshire.

Surrey heathland was well suited to hunting and at one time the county was afforested as far south as the Guildford Downs. Forest Law was greatly resented by the English population - Robin Hood has passed down in legend for his opposition to the repressive forest laws at this time. Magna Carta, which King John was compelled to sign by the barons in 1215, included some sanctions to curb the extension and jurisdiction of Forest Law. In 1327 Edward II granted a charter excluding all of Surrey from forest jurisdiction but nevertheless retained a 'purlieu' (special hunting rights) to the deer in this part of northwest Surrey.

an offence punishable by death. Commoners living in afforested areas were accorded some special exemptions from Forest Law, for example the right to collect fuel and limited grazing for their animals. These rights are

FRIMLEY GREEN, OLD COTTAGE 1906 54907

THE BASING STONE 2004 C12705k (Hazelle Jackson)

Near the Jolly Farmer roundabout, where the ancient Maultway track crosses the A30 road, a roadside stone links the hunting forests of the past to the present day. Stapled to a boulder, a faded metal plaque reads: 'SITE OF THE BASING STONE AND LEGEND OF THE WHITE HART'. (The original stone probably 'disappeared' when road works were carried out in the 1950s).

According to the legend, it was near the Basingstone (Beausantstone) that Richard II (1377 –1399) was attacked by a wounded stag while out hunting and saved by a white hart that came between them. In gratitude the King is said to have caused four hostelries with the sign of the White Hart to be erected in the forest at Bagshot, Chobham, Frimley, and Pirbright. Of these only the White Hart Inns at Frimley and Pirbright still exist and the one at Pirbright is now called the Moorhen. (The current White Hart at Bagshot is a later building – the original White Hart was demolished in 1949 and there are now offices on the site.)

Although Forest Law restricted the growth of many local industries, there is evidence that gravel and sand were quarried from Bagshot Heath in the Middle Ages and in places south of the Blackwater river, thick veins of yellow clay were used to make a distinctive pottery known as Border Ware which was exported across Europe as late as the end of the 18th century.

Up to the middle of the 16th century, the Great West Road (today's A30) was not the main thoroughfare for traffic between London to the West Country. In 1571 however the first references appear in contemporary documents to a road across Bagshot Heath in north-west Surrey leading to Basingstoke and Salisbury and on to Exeter. This road crossed the Blackwater river at the county boundary with Hampshire and Berkshire where the A30 does today and the river was forded here. Blackwater was a changing point for coaches and horses and had two alehouses and three large coaching inns, one of which had its own brewery.

Before the development of modern Camberley, for centuries Frimley was the largest settlement in the Blackwater Valley. There are records of Queen Mary holding court in the White Hart Inn, which still stands at the top of Frimley High Street today.

FRIMLEY 1901 46835

A granddaughter of John White, owner of the Manor of Frimley in the sixteenth century, married Sir Walter Tichborne in 1602 and their descendents James and Mary Tichborne, the sixth generation of the family to own the estate, built the present mansion, Frimley Park Manor House, in around 1710 on the site of a modest hunting lodge. The Manor of Frimley owned much of the land in Frimley Heath. The house and estate changed hands in the late 18th century when the last of the Tichbournes to live there sold Frimley Park Manor house and lands to James Laurell in around 1790.

Did you know?

Frimley Manor

On the dissolution of the monasteries, Henry VIII gave the Frimley Manor estate to his daughter Mary and when she became Queen in 1553 she gave it to Sir John White of Aldershot, as a reward for his service as Lord Mayor of London.

The Jolly Farmer

'The Jolly Farmer' inn was once called 'The Golden Farmer', the nickname for highwayman William Davis who lived nearby in the 17th Century. William Davis (1627-1690) was a notorious villain who roamed Bagshot Heath in the seventeenth century. Born in Wrexham he moved with his wife and family to Bagshot in Surrey where he became a farmer. To supplement his income he turned to highway robbery mainly on Bagshot Heath but also as far afield as Salisbury Plain. Operating alone he became famous as a master of disguise, at one time robbing his own landlord of the annual rent money just collected from him. Nicknamed the 'Golden Farmer' because of his prompt payment of debts, usually in gold, he continued his life of crime - supposedly without his wife's knowledge - for forty years until 1690 when aged sixty-four he was shot and captured during a coach hold-up. He was hanged in London 1690.

WILLIAM DAVIS, THE 'GOLDEN FARMER' ZZZ01302

The wild and uncompromising nature of the land and the lack of habitation meant that from the 16th to the 18th centuries travellers on the Great West Road literally took their life in their hands. Many gentlemen travelled with large pistols and cudgels for self-protection from highwaymen and bandits who laid in wait in the scrub to catch unwary travellers.

There are other roads in the area which commemorate the lawlessness of Bagshot Heath at this time: Snow's Ride in Windlesham, is named after Captain Snow who roamed Bagshot Heath in the 18th century and Gibbet Hill recalls where captured highwaymen were hung and their bodies left to swing in the wind as a warning to others of their kind.

Bagshot Heath lay mainly to the north of the Great West Road. To the south lay Frimley Heath. This was bounded by the Blackwater river in the west and Chobham Ridge and the Maultway in the East. At its southern end was the village of Frimley.

From the Tudor period the Great West Road (A30) was the main route for postal communications with the West of England. The first postal service was established by Henry VIII, who contracted innkeepers to maintain the changes of horses for his dispatch riders, along the six main designated post roads from London. Post-boys carried letters in relays from inn to inn and over time innkeepers also took to carrying private letters, a practice legalised in 1635 with a proclamation from King Charles I, from Bagshot Park, allowing the public to use his "Royal Mail". Postmasters, who were in charge of posthouses, had two main responsibilities: to receive and forward mail and to deliver letters in their own district, and to hire out horses and guides for travellers along the same relay system (the travelling-post). The mail was to be carried at the rate of six miles an hour. To be found loitering on the road was to be committed to the House of Correction and to be confined with hard labour for a month.

THE JOLLY FARMER 1906 57182p

By 1660 regular coach services were travelling from London to the west and south-west, calling in at Bagshot and Blackwater which expanded rapidly as coaching towns at this time. But the Great West Road, in common with all British roads in the early 17th century, was often a quagmire of mud and impassable at certain times of year.

The major reason for the decline in road conditions in the millennium after the Romans left was that local parishes were charged with repairing the roads in their own parish. Poor parishes had no funds to do this and for centuries the roads decayed throughout the British Isles.

Finally in an effort to improve the roads, from 1663 onwards, Parliament passed legislation allowing companies to build and maintain toll roads. Also from 1697 signposts could be required to be erected - previously travellers on the long-distance highways often took strip maps to follow their route and determine where to turn off the road for a branch road. After George I came to the throne in 1714 there was a great improvement in communications across the country as Turnpike Trusts were set up to establish tolls to take the maintenance of major roadways out of the hands of impoverished parishes.

Turnpike Trusts raised revenue by charging tolls to road users which they collected from tollbooths at each end of a turnpiked stretch of road. In 1728 the Bedfont and Bagshot Turnpike Trust was responsible for the Great West Road from the Hounslow

BLACKWATER BRIDGE 1901 46816

Powder Mills to the Basingstone near the Jolly Farmer today. There was another tollgate at Three Post Boys Inn at the western end of Camberley near the Blackwater river crossing.

In 1780 the letting of horses was thrown open to the public and any establishment

could call itself a posting house. The mail service however remained painfully slow. In 1782 the Post Office took 38 hours to send mail from London to Bath, a distance of some 109 miles, via post boys or couriers. A letter posted on Monday in London would reach Bath only by Wednesday and no reply was possible in London until Saturday (at the earliest). (In the light of the current problems being experienced by the Royal Mail some readers may think that things are little better today). The mail too was regularly robbed by the many thieves along the road.

Did you know?

Milestones

The Romans erected the earliest milestones but like their roads this fell into disuse after they left the British Isles in the fifth century. They reappeared as staging posts for the Royal Mail riders and were used to measure progress. When the Turnpike Trusts took over road maintenance they erected many of the milestones we still see by the road today. Milestones came in a variety of sizes and the triangular one shown in the photo, in the Yorktown end of Camberley measured from each direction on the faces on each side.

LONDON ROAD MILESTONE 2004
C12706k (Hazelle Jackson)

This sorry state of affairs prompted John Palmer, a theatre manager in the West Country, to stage a demonstration of just how fast it was possible to deliver the mail. On Monday 2 August 1784 he staged an experiment in which he proved the journey from London to Bristol could be done in 16 hours by a high-speed coach. After some initial grumpiness from the Post Office, Palmer's concept was adopted and this ushered in the age of the Mail coach.

Soon the toll roads of England rang to the sound of thundering horses' hoofs. All traffic, including soldiers on the road, had to give way to the Mail coach as it sounded its horn and it must have been akin to a police car with sirens howling when the mail coaches, in their distinctive red and black livery, thundered down the main roads and through the turnpike during the night as well as the day. It was the guard's responsibility to get the mail through - if the mail coach's wheels got stuck in the mud, then the guards could take the horses and ride on. If they couldn't ride they were expected to take the mail to the next stage on foot. Every mail coach carried its own 'repair' kit to carry out simple repairs on the road and coaching towns had inns, smithies, stables and fresh horses.

A local landmark, which would have been familiar to the stage and mail coaches on the Bagshot Turnpike would have been the Camberley 'obelisk'. This is an 18th century tower, standing today on a hill behind Surrey Heath council offices and virtually hidden in the middle of a modern housing development. Until the early 20th century, before the present

Did you know?

The Obelisk

In the 18th century John Norris Esquire resided at Hawley Manor House. Norris was a friend of Sir Francis Dashwood of West Wycombe, and a member of the notorious Hell Fire club. The two men also shared an interest in horse racing and Sir Francis is known to have stabled his horses at Hawley Manor's stables.

In the 1770s Mr Norris built a large signalling tower, known as the Obelisk, on a hill just behind where the modern Surrey Heath Council offices are today. The tower was largely burnt down in a fire in the 1880s but it has been suggested that originally it had a roof lantern which may have been lit to guide night-time hunts. (Stags rest during the day and feed at night which was when they were hunted). Another possible use which has been suggested, although the signalling system used is unclear, is that Mr Norris and Sir Francis may have used the top of the tower to exchange racing tips - flashing the information from the top of the Obelisk to a room in the 'golden ball' on the top of the church on the hill at West Wycombe.

THE CAMBERLEY OBELISK 2004 C12707k (Hazelle Jackson)

Over the years the tower decayed and fell into disuse and out of view in the grounds of The Knoll, a house built nearby. Now a Grade II listed building it was opened to the public once more when the land around it was incorporated into Camberley Park to celebrate the Millennium.

COACHING PRINT F6021

trees cover in the area, it would have been visible from a long distance.

Stage and mail coaches carried both people and parcels, with many travellers preferring the speed and relative security of the mail coach even though it meant an uncomfortable ride through the night. Larger and bulkier items went by packhorse

trains which were still a common sight on highways and were the most reliable form of moving goods - each animal could carry up to 180kg and the packhorse train cover up to 40kms per day.

Then the Duke of Bridgewater built the first canal and demonstrated how effective canals could be for transporting heavy goods. Canal mania followed in the 1760s and 1770s. All over the country companies were set up to construct inland waterways as backers competed to make their fortunes from canal speculation. In Surrey and Hampshire the Basingstoke Canal was proposed in the 18th century to develop the already thriving agricultural trade of central Hampshire. Basingstoke, an established market centre was chosen as the terminus for a 37-mile long canal, which would link to the Thames

STAGECOACH ZZZ01303

via a 3-mile length of the Wey Navigation, and create a 70-mile waterway to the Pool of London. This opened in 1794.

The Basingstoke canal was not a commercial success. Trade to London consisted mainly of malt, flour and timber and the owners established fir plantations along the Canal as an additional source of income. Most of the trade from London was in coal and groceries while the main local traffic was in timber and chalk. However the canal played an important role in transporting materials for the construction of the military establishments at Camberley, Aldershot and North Camp, which were built locally in the 19th century.

The Basingstoke Canal

Construction of the canal began in 1778, took six years, and included the building of 29 locks, a 1,230-yard long tunnel through Greywell Hill and the 50-yard Little Tunnel Bridge at Mapledurwell, 69 bridges, five lock houses, four wharves and three warehouses. The canal came west out of Woking to Frimley Green where it turned south towards Basingstoke. The mile-long cutting at Deepcut and the 1,000-yard long Ash Embankment across the Blackwater Valley were completed in an astonishingly short time by navvies equipped with little more than wheelbarrows, picks and shovels. (Restoration of the canal, starting in the mid 1970s, took 16 years!) The canal was constructed to allow passage of craft up to 72ft long and 13ft wide and was opened on 4 September 1794.

FRIMLEY GREEN, THE CANAL 1909 61829x

FRIMLEY GREEN, THE LOCK 1906 54914

STAFF COLLEGE 1901 46829p

CHAPTER TWO

Military Manoeuvres

ROYAL MILITARY COLLEGE 1895 35157a

THE FIRST military training college for British army officers was the Royal Military Academy (the RMA) which was founded in 1741, by Royal Warrant from George II. It was located in a large military complex at Woolwich known as The Warren.

Until 1855 the Royal Regiment of Artillery and the all-officer corps of Royal Engineers remained, except for operational purposes, under the control of the Master General of the Ordnance, and were quite separate from the rest of the British army.

The RMA, known as 'the Shop' to generations of its graduates, trained officers in the artillery regiments (and later engineers and signallers), collectively known as the Ordnance Corps. Historically the 'artillery' covered all the major technical roles in the army and entry was by examination. All

Second Lieutenants in the Ordnance Corps had to pass the RMA course as gentlemen cadets in order to be commissioned and there was strong competition for commissions as the work was regarded as interesting and rewarding.

So when did Sandhurst enter the scene?

Until 1877 officers in the British army, outside the Ordnance Corps, purchased their commissions on payment of a lump sum and were not required to pass any entrance examinations nor undergo tests of suitability for a military career.

The Army was a favoured career for younger sons, who were unlikely to inherit the main family estate but had the means to buy a commission. (Fans of Jane Austen's 'Pride and Prejudice' will recall that Mr Darcy purchased a new commission for the dastardly Mr

BROADMOOR PAINTING ZZZ01304

Wickham, in a distant Northern regiment, after Wickham was forced to resign his existing commission when he eloped with Lydia Bennett to avoid his gambling debts).

Once commissioned there was no formal training for these officers, it was assumed they would learn their skills 'on the job'. The war with France between 1793-1815 highlighted the shortcomings of this system and in the late 1790s a career officer, Colonel John Gaspard Le Marchant, who had the ear of George III, drew up plans for formal training for all officers not in the Ordnance Corps. He proposed setting up a Royal Military College (the RMC) consisting of three sections: a Senior Department to train officers in staff duties, a Junior Department, similar to the RMA, to train gentlemen cadets to be junior officers and the Legion, made up of the sons of non-commissioned officers who would be educated to become NCOs. With the support of the Duke of York, who was made Commander-in-Chief of the army in 1798, the plans went ahead.

In 1799 a school for officers was established at High Wycombe in Buckinghamshire with Le Marchant at its first Commandant; in 1801 this was designated the Senior Department of the new Royal Military College. In 1802 a Junior Department was set up in Great Marlow, also in Buckinghamshire, to train gentlemen officer cadets for commissions in the Cavalry and Infantry. The accommodation chosen for these colleges proved unsuitable for military training and the search began for a new site for a purpose-built Royal Military College. The

ROYAL MILITARY ACADEMY 1901 46822

Old College, Sandhurst

The original RMC College building was designed in neo-classical style by one of the leading architects of the day, James Wyatt (who also designed the RMA building at Woolwich). The Old College, as it is now called, took eleven years to build although the first six were spent on construction of the bricks, most of which were found on first inspection to be substandard. The contractor, Mr Alexander Copland, was

voted further sums to finish the work, and the materials were brought up via the newly built Basingstoke canal to Frimley Wharf a few miles to the south. The Royal Military College was finally completed in 1812 at a cost of £365,000.

KING'S WALK, ROYAL MILITARY ACADEMY c1955 C12010

location eventually chosen was Sandhurst on the borders of Berkshire and Surrey.

At this time Sandhurst was a small farming community near the Blackwater River on the edge of Windsor Forest to the north of the Great West Road. In the late seventeenth century a local farmer, Richard Lodge, had enclosed a 450-acre site from the forest, and established a farm and mill there. (A local brook, the Wish Stream, a tributary of the Blackwater River fed the mill ponds.) This estate was called Sandhurst Park.

In 1799 the executors of the Lodge estate sold Sandhurst Park to John Tekel (or Tekell), a former army officer from Yorkshire who purchased it with money raised from selling his commission on leaving the army. (This was a common way for retiring officers to raise money). The rundown estate cost

him around £2000 and, according to one contemporary account, Tekel had plans to fertilise the poor quality soil with horse dung from the streets of London.

In 1800 Tekel married Lady Griselda Stanhope, the niece of the Prime Minister William Pitt the Younger (1759-1806). Shortly afterwards, he sold the Sandhurst estate to Pitt for a small profit. In 1801 Pitt in turn sold it to the Treasury for £8,000, to be the site for the new Royal Military College. Some commentators have suggested that Pitt made a financial killing on the deal. The truth is sadder. Pitt was a bachelor, who was notoriously inept at running his household, regularly cheated on by his servants and constantly in debt. In February 1801 he resigned as Prime Minister after a disagreement with King

George III over the Act of Union with Ireland. When he lost his job he also lost his Prime Minister's salary. Without private means his financial position was so bad that it seemed likely he might be made bankrupt: he owed £45,000 and was forced to sell his houses. Friends rallied round in 1802 to help but even the profit he made on the sale of his property including the Sandhurst estate, did little more than stave off the worst of his creditors. His health, always delicate, had been seriously weakened by years of excessive port drinking, (a 'cure' recommended by his doctor for his inherited gout, when he was only 14,) and the anxiety of the continuing war with France. Despite the care of his niece, the explorer Lady Hester Stanhope, (Lady Griselda's sister), he died in 1806, at the age of 46, probably from renal failure and cirrhosis of the liver. Parliament voted £40,000 to settle his outstanding debts, pensions were granted to his three nieces, including Lady Griselda and a public funeral was held in Westminster Abbey.

Sandhurst was now set to be the location for the new Royal Military College. It had a number of attractions in the eyes of the authorities: it was far enough away from London to prevent cadets becoming 'distracted' by the bright lights of the city but on the main London road at a convenient distance from the capital. It was also near to Windsor Castle, home to the Royal Family and to Colonel le Marchant's family home at Chobham. The vast surrounding heathland was suitable for military manoeuvres.

Did you know?

Barossa

Large parts of the Sandhurst site were left in their original state as training grounds. The area to the east of the main college building was named 'Barossa' by the early RMC staff because of its supposed resemblance to a battle site in the Peninsular War in the Iberian peninsula (1808-14).

BAROSSA, OLD DEAN COMMON 1931 83859

ROYAL STAFF COLLEGE 1919 68798

The original site purchased from Pitt was increased by the purchase and enclosure of adjacent land, and work began on landscaping the main grounds, designed by Mr Bracebridge, a follower of Capability Brown. The Wish Stream millponds were excavated by troops and local civilian labour and turned into today's ornamental lakes. The soil from the excavation was used to level the exercise ground and parade square. It was estimated that 3,500 cartloads were removed from the site when they excavated the lakes at Sandhurst RMC, at 6d a load.

In 1811 Colonel Le Marchant visited the site to inspect progress and remarked to his son that, '...it was here at Sandhurst he could expect to pass the remainder of his days'. This was clearly tempting fate for a soldier and soon afterwards he was promoted to Major-General and sent to join Wellington in Spain where a year later he was killed leading the cavalry charge which secured the great British victory at Salamanca.

The transfer of the RMC Junior department from its premises in Great Marlow was speeded-up after a visit by the Prince Regent in 1811 when he was heard to observe, 'I would rather like this for a palace!' The first official Royal visit took place in the summer of 1813 when the Prince Regent and his brother the Duke of York came to present the first Colours. Both managed to get hopelessly drunk.

The RMC's Senior Department moved to Farnham in 1814 and then to Sandhurst in 1821.

The Staff College

The Staff College was designed by government architect Sir James Pennethorne in the style of a French chateau, and built on the eastern edge of the Sandhurst site. The building of the new Staff College commenced in 1860 when Queen Victoria and Prince Albert planted a beech tree on the front lawn. Prince Albert is believed to have caught the typhoid which led to his death in 1861 while on a visit to Sandhurst to inspect the building work on the new Staff College.

In 1856 the Duke of Cambridge became Commander-in-Chief at the end of the Crimean war and further changes took place in officer training. In 1858 the Senior Department was renamed as the Staff College with a remit to run a two year course with entrance and final exams devised for staff officers. The Staff College opened in 1862, (the same year as the Broadmoor Asylum for the Criminally Insane just north of the RMC at Crowthorne in Berkshire.)

Until 1858 the Indian sub-continent was administered by the East India Company who maintained their own military establishment. Recognising early on the need to train its soldiers, the East India Company had at first sent its cadets to train at the RMA at Woolwich in 1798 and then in 1809 set up its own military seminary at Addiscombe House, Croydon, based upon the RMA Woolwich model. After the Indian Mutiny of 1857-8, it was decided that all artillery and engineers in India should be part of the British Army and the numbers of students studying at the

Sandhurst received a further boost. The East India Company's military training college at Addiscombe was closed and all candidates for the Indian Staff Corps had first to serve for two years on probation as subalterns in the British Army. Those who did not wish to purchase commissions in the British Army prior to joining the Indian Staff Corps were able to attend the Royal Military College at Sandhurst instead.

Throughout most of the 19th century the purchase system for commissions was still in force but gentlemen cadets who completed the RMC course and were recommended by the College authorities could be granted their first commissions without purchase. When there were more candidates than vacancies, RMC cadets were given priority.

Despite its many apparent advantages the RMC at Sandhurst gained a reputation for disorderly behaviour, rioting and bullying exacerbated by the petty rules imposed on the gentlemen officer cadets who studied there. Their frustration eventually boiled over in the Cadet Mutiny of 1862 when the cadet battalion withstood a three-day siege in

Did you know?
Beer

Simonds of Reading was awarded the contract to supply beer to the Royal Military College at Sandhurst in 1814. This led to them being made suppliers of beer to the army world-wide.

NEW COLLEGE, SANDHURST 2004 C12708k (Hazelle Jackson)

one of the earthworks used for fortification training. They finally surrendered to the Duke of Cambridge, who came down in his coach from London to restore order.

In 1870 in an endeavour to modernise the recruitment methods, the purchase system for commissions in the army was abolished and commissions were awarded by written competitive examination. During this time the RMC closed and the buildings were used to train successful candidates in military skills while they waited to join their regiments. However this system did not provide the desired results and in 1877 the examination became one for appointment to the RMC

as a cadet, rather than for a commission. In practice the cost of the college fees was much the same as that formerly charged for an ensign's commission, and this, plus the school fees required to prepare for the entry examinations, meant that the social composition of the Army's officers remained unchanged.

By now the RMC was not large enough to train all the subalterns needed by the Army, so an alternative route arose, favoured by those who failed entry to the College, to obtain a commission by nomination in the Militia. It was then possible to transfer to the Regular Army after a period of full-time service and passing the College's final examination. The Army remained a popular career choice with younger sons in aristocratic families. Sir Winston Churchill (1874-95) was educated at Harrow and then Sandhurst. He was admitted to Sandhurst at his third attempt in 1893 and commissioned as a second lieutenant in the 4th Hussar Regiment in February 1895. He resigned his commission in 1899 and was taken prisoner while reporting the Boer War in South Africa but escaped and returned to England where in 1900 he was elected as Conservative MP for Oldham.

Following the setbacks of the Boer War in the late nineteenth century, the army was increased in size at the start of the 20th century and the New College, an imposing red brick building, was built on the Sandhurst site to accommodate the increased numbers. This opened in 1912. It was designed by H B Measures, Director of Barrack Construction and built by T. Rowbotham of Birmingham, at a cost of £105,000.

Throughout the 19th and first half of the 20th century students at the Royal Military Academy, Woolwich and the Royal Military College, Sandhurst, continued to be known as gentlemen cadets. This meant that, unlike modern Officer Cadets, who are technically private soldiers and are paid and clothed by the MOD, gentlemen cadets were not subject to military law. Their parents paid tuition and boarding fees, in the same way as at a public school or university, and also paid for uniforms, books, and equipment.

Fees were reduced for the sons of serving or former officers, and there were also a number of cadetships (comparable to scholarships). Admission was by competitive written examination in a variety of academic subjects, and candidates passed, in order of merit, according to the number of marks they achieved. There were no practical tests of aptitude for leadership - these were first introduced during the Second World - and this system had the effect of favouring entry towards public schoolboys with the means to afford the training and often from families with a military connection.

Both the RMA and RMC were closed when war was declared in September 1939 and Sandhurst then became the home of 161 Infantry Officer Cadet Training Unit. This unit moved to Mons Barracks, Aldershot in 1942 and for the rest of the war Sandhurst was used solely as a Royal Armoured Corps Officer Cadet training Unit. Although Camberley did not suffer to the same extent as London during the war a number of warplanes did find their way through. On the night of 29th January 1941 a German aircraft dropped a stick of bombs on New College, killing five cadets.

After the Second World War a major restructuring of officer training took place. In 1947 the Royal Military Academy Sandhurst was established by merging the Royal Military Academy, Woolwich and the Royal Military College, Sandhurst. The combined academy was located at Sandhurst and the motto chosen for the new establishment was 'Serve to Lead', emphasising the leadership

Did you know?

David Niven

David Niven, the Hollywood film star in the 1940s, 50s and 60s was born into a military family in 1910 (the son of a British Army lieutenant who died at Gallipoli in 1915). He attended Sandhurst from 1928-30 and was commissioned into the Highland Light Infantry in 1930. He resigned his commission and moved to Hollywood in 1935 to try his hand at acting. His witty and urbane style soon saw him rising through the ranks to become a star. When the Second World War broke out he returned to the UK and joined the Rifle Brigade. By the end of the war Niven had worked his way up to the rank of Lieutenant Colonel in the British Commandos, including some time in Normandy during the invasion. After the war, he was made a Legionnaire of the Order of Merit (the highest American order that can be bestowed on a non-citizen) which was presented to him personally by General Dwight D. Eisenhower. He returned to Hollywood after the war, achieving major success in the 1950s and won an Oscar for his performance in Separate Tables (1958). A major star for over four decades, he became a best selling author in the 1970s with his autobiographies "The Moon's a Balloon" and "Bring on the Empty Horses". He died from a neurological disorder in 1983.

DAVID NIVEN ZZZ01305

Niven is seen here in 'Enchantment' with Teresa May in 1949.

role of the officer class and replacing the Latin 'Sua Tela Tonanti' ('Their weapons are Thunderbolts') of the RMA and 'Vires Aquirit Eundo' ('It gains strength as it goes') of the RMC.

The Royal Military Academy, Sandhurst was formally established in 1947 by the amalgamation of the Royal Military Academy, Woolwich and the Royal Military College, Sandhurst.

Officer cadets, now employed by the Ministry of Defence, were given a university level training which lasted eighteen months, later increased to two years. The course included the traditional military subjects such as drill, infantry tactics, skill-at-arms, and field craft, with an emphasis on the development of leadership skills. There was a strong academic element taught by civilian lecturers.

Following the Second World War military conscription rules were changed and all fit males, on reaching their eighteenth birthday, were required to serve up to two years with the colours followed by three in the Territorial Army or other part-time Reserves. Those who wished to do so could volunteer for three years as Short Service Regular soldiers, with better pay and conditions. National Service and Short Service commissions were available to provide the large numbers of junior officers required by a large army, but as both categories were only engaged for a limited period, Officer Cadet training for Short Service commissions was restricted to a few months.

PASSING OUT PARADE, MONS BARRACKS ZZZ01306

BAROSSA, OLD DEAN COMMON 1931 83859

Two Officer Cadet Schools were set up for Short Service commissions: at Mons Barracks, in nearby Aldershot (the garrison headquarters of the British army) and at Eaton Hall, Cheshire. Officer Cadets of the Royal Armoured Corps or Royal Artillery went to Mons while those of the other arms and services went to Eaton Hall.

National Service was abolished in 1960 but the Short Service commission route was retained. Eaton Hall OCS was closed and Mons Officer Cadet School took over training all Short Service Officer Cadets, and all graduate recruits to the Regular Army. As the supply of ex-National Service officers dwindled, Mons also undertook the final training of candidates for Territorial Army commissions.

The intensive training system at Mons proved very popular with recruits, because the training was shorter and they could be commissioned in six months, while the top brass appreciated the speed and relative cheapness of the Mons training system. In 1972 Mons OCS moved from Aldershot to the New College building at Sandhurst where it took over all Officer cadet training.

During the Second World War the Women's Royal Army Corps came to play an increasingly important role in the modern army. In 1948 an Officer School of Instruction for the WRAC was opened at Huron Camp in Hindhead in Surrey. In 1951 the War Department took over Frimley Park Manor House, just south of Camberley, for the

STAFF COLLEGE 2004 C12709k (Hazelle Jackson)

OLD COLLEGE 2004 C12711k (Hazelle Jackson)

WRAC staff college which remained there until 1957. WRAC Officers first attended the Army Staff College at Camberley in 1962.

In 1965 a WRAC Officer College was built on the site of the former Royal Albert Orphanage and School three miles away east of Sandhurst. Inevitably it made sense to share some training in academic subjects and by mid 1970, joint training in academic subjects was taking place. In 1981 the WRAC College was incorporated as the 4th College of RMA Sandhurst and in 1984, WRAC officer cadets and student officers moved to Old College RMA Sandhurst as the WRAC.

Today female officer cadets make up around 10% of the intake and the cadets do much of their training side by side.

In 1997 the Ministry of Defence created the Joint Services Command and Staff College (JSCSC) for all the military services and built a new building for the college at Shrivenham in Wiltshire. This opened in 2002 enabling all military command and staff training for the forces to be delivered from one site. As a result the Staff College building was vacated at Sandhurst. Today it is home to number of army support services including the Army Management Consultancy Services, Management Accountancy Services (Army), the Army Medical Directorate (Medico-Legal) and the Army Medical Services Headquarters Officers' Mess.

In 2004 the Royal Military Academy at Sandhurst trains officer cadets from all over the world, including countries from the former Eastern bloc.

The Commissioning Course takes 44 weeks and provides initial training for all future officers of the regular army, including expeditions and specialist training for infantry, artillery, logistics and other technical or general arms training. Many distinguished soldiers and heads of state have taken part in the famous Sandhurst passing out parade where the Adjutant rides his horse up the steps of the Old College. They include many members of the Jordanian Royal family (including the first Arab princess, Princess Ayesha of Jordan) and of the Bahraini and Dubai ruling families.

Staff at the RMAS are mindful of the need to develop and evolve their courses and to equip officers with the skills appropriate to the modern business world outside the army. Since April 1997 in addition to receiving their commissions, cadets have been eligible to hold licentiate membership of the Institute of Personnel and Development (now the Chartered IPD). In 2003 the RMAS announced further accreditations including Associate level membership of the Chartered Management Institute and a Licentiate in Leadership from the City and Guilds Institute.

In 2004 there was a full complement of 1000 officer cadets undergoing training including 100 females officer cadets. Courses at the RMAS have never been more in demand to provide professional officers for armies all around the world. In June 2004 it was announced that Prince Harry, third in line to the British throne, intended to take up a career in the army after training at Sandhurst in 2005.

OLD COLLEGE 2004 (Hazelle Jackson)

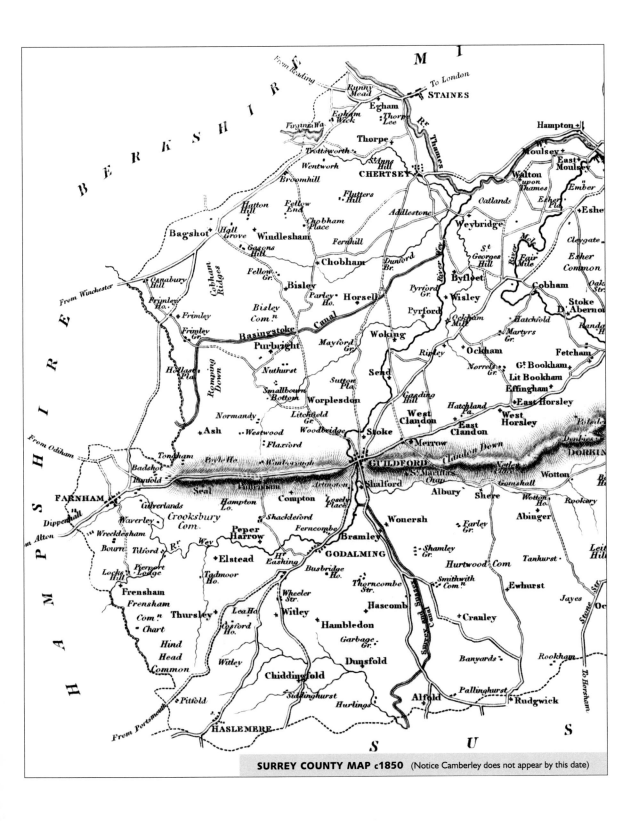

SURREY COUNTY MAP c1850 (Notice Camberley does not appear by this date)

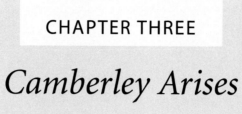

CHAPTER THREE

Camberley Arises

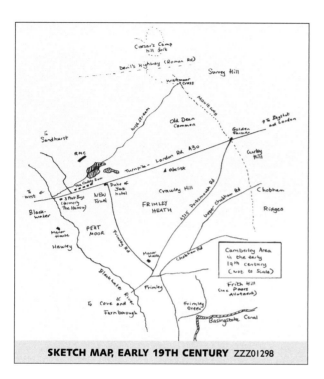

SKETCH MAP, EARLY 19TH CENTURY ZZZ01298

IN 1800 James Laurell was the owner of the Frimley Manor estate which included Frimley Park Manor House and around 1,315 acres of land. A restless and ambitious man he saw an opportunity to considerably increase his land holdings with Frimley Enclosure Act of 1801.

The Enclosure Acts were passed to rationalise land ownership and make it more productive by distributing the former common land to the rich in the hope that they would improve it and increase food production. Not surprisingly many landowners who acquired land in this way later sold it for development or to other landowners wanting to increase their estates. The rules on entitlement to claim land, which were complex, were administered by Enclosure commissioners but as Lord of the Manor of Frimley and a substantial local landowner,

Laurell was clearly able to make a convincing case and doubled his estate to over 3,500 acres acquiring great swathes of land across Frimley Heath, Old Dean Common and the high ground up to Chobham Ridges to the east.

In the years after the Enclosure Acts there was considerable hardship to many rural communities who no longer had access to common land for fuel and food. In Frimley many villagers became destitute and the authorities built a workhouse where Tomlinscote School is now situated. The Enclosure Commissioners were then required to set aside a portion of common land to provide a supply of fuel for poorer families. The Frimley Poors Allotment Act set aside a parcel of 350 acres of land near Frith Hill to the east of Frimley for this purpose. In 1826 the Frimley Fuel Allotments charity was set up to ensure the poor benefited from the allotments, in a measure replicated in many districts around the country. The surviving land from this allotment is still known today as the Frimley Fuel Allotments.

Soon after expanding his estate, Laurell started to plant fir trees on the Colling Ridge on the western side of the Maultway, starting some of the first fir plantations in the area. Further planting took place in the Heatherside and Crawley Ridge areas in the 1820s and these trees soon spread further afield and south into the Frimley Fuel Allotments area. These provided further sources of fuel to the villagers entitled to collect and this practice, in turn, helped to preserved the heathland.

OLD COTTAGE 1906 57181

Tea Caddy Row

In 1805 a local brewer, William Parfett from Eversley, who owned The Three Post Boys (formerly the Harrow), a coaching inn on the London Road near the Blackwater turnpike, purchased a strip of land between the Wish stream on the north side of the London Road from James Laurell. He promptly sold this to the government who built a row of smart Regency houses there for the officers and senior teaching staff at the Royal Military College at Sandhurst. These houses, which today are listed buildings, were christened Tea Caddy Row, after their boxy shape, by the coachmen driving up and down the turnpike road.

THE TERRACE, ROYAL MILITARY COLLEGE 1901 46825

Mr Parfett clearly knew a business opportunity when he saw one. In 1816 he built a smart new hotel on the corner of London Road and Frimley Road which he named the 'Duke of York' after the Commander-in-Chief of the British Army. The hotel offered accommodation to relatives visiting the gentlemen cadets at the college and refreshment to students and workmen. Today it is a local landmark and one of the oldest surviving commercial buildings in Camberley.

The laying-out of the grounds of the Royal Military College and the construction of the college itself, between 1802-1812, also presented business opportunities. Buildings materials for the college were brought up the Basingstoke canal to Frimley Wharf and up Frimley Road, past the 'Duke of York' to the college itself.

The workmen employed on the site needed housing and supplies and a small community of workmen and college staff soon grew up along the London Road here and a number of shops opened to serve them. A Baptist chapel and a National School joined the burgeoning community in the early years of the 19th century, which was known at first as New Town.

In 1837 John and Lady Griselda Tekel, (the original owners of the Sandhurst Park estate in 1799), purchased the original Frimley Manor

Did you know?

York Town

The Yorktown district of Camberley was originally called New Town. It was renamed York Town (Yorktown) in 1831 in honour of the Duke of York, who was the Commander-in-Chief of the Army.

LONDON ROAD, THE DUKE OF YORK HOTEL 1931 83847

estate from James Laurell and moved into Frimley Park Manor house. Local legend has it that Tekel won the house and estate from Laurell in a game of cards at which the Prince of Wales was present. The story goes that Tekel strode in one night while Laurell was at dinner to claim his prize. Entertaining as this notion of Regency rakes gambling all on the turn of a card may be, it does not appear to be true.

Research in the 1980s by Camberley historian Gordon Wellard, at the Surrey County Records office at Kingston, reveals a different story. In 1806 Laurell sold Frimley Park Manor House and much of the original estate between London Road and Portsmouth Road, to John Tekel for £22,000. Tekel made a down payment of £7,000 but it seems to have taken him a further 21 years, until 1837, to raise the remaining £15,000. John and Lady Griselda then moved in to Frimley Park Manor House doubtless fulfilling a long held ambition to live there. Laurell moved to Eastwick Park near Bookham. Lady Griselda Tekel died in 1851 and John Tekel died in 1858. There were no children of the marriage and in 1859 their executors put their estate up for sale. It was described in the sale particulars of the time as: 'The Frimley Park Estate: A residential property with a domain of 1,457 aces presenting fine sporting features in a most excellent neighbourhood'. Among the features mentioned in the sale particulars are:

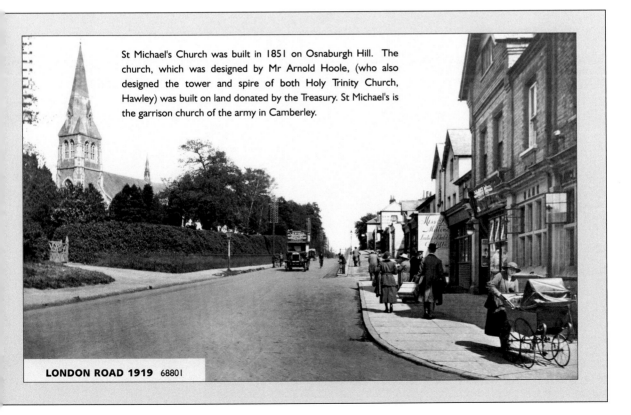

St Michael's Church was built in 1851 on Osnaburgh Hill. The church, which was designed by Mr Arnold Hoole, (who also designed the tower and spire of both Holy Trinity Church, Hawley) was built on land donated by the Treasury. St Michael's is the garrison church of the army in Camberley.

LONDON ROAD 1919 68801

HIGH STREET 1901 46833

'Thriving plantations of larch and Scotch fir' on the Bristow and Park farms (to the south and west of the estate). There was also 'A large tract of land with valuable plantation belted by Scots firs of large size giving the estate some very beautiful features (Tekell's Park) within a ring fence 1,457 acres'. This was the area planted in 1802 by James Laurell along the estate's eastern boundary. We also know that the Tekels had a hunting lodge on Crawley Ridge.

In the 1850s the Crimean War came to an end and in 1856 the Duke of Cambridge was appointed Commander-in-Chief of the British Army. This led to a review of the training given to staff officers and it was decided to replace the Senior Department of the Royal Military College with a designated specialist staff college. Work started on the army Staff College at Sandhurst in 1859, which coincided with the Frimley Park estate going up for sale on the death of John Tekel.

Local developers were not slow to spot the opening this created. Although the sale of the estate was announced for May 1860, it was in fact sold in February that year by private treaty to Edwin Newman of Yeovil for £32,500. The area sold covered the land from the Frimley Park Manor house, up to the London Road, west to the Blackwater River in the west and east to the Portsmouth Road. Very soon afterwards, in June 1860, Mr Newman sold the Frimley Manor estate to Captain Knight of Esher and his brother-in-law Major Spring of West Molesey. If

anyone can be called the founder of modern Camberley then it must be Captain Knight. The two men divided the estate into two parts along Park Street and set about developing it. (Captain Knight took the Manor house and the eastern side while Major Spring took the western sector.

Captain Knight built himself a large new house on the site of the Tekels' old hunting lodge on Crawley Hill in the 1860s and called it, after the castellated style of its architecture, Tekell's Castle. When it was ready for occupation he sold Frimley Park Manor house and some of the grounds to Sir William Stansfield.

It soon became clear to Captain Knight and Major Spring that to attract residents (and investors) they needed a railway station serving York Town and Cambridge Town. The railway had already arrived in the surrounding area: a station was built at Farnborough in 1838 on the London & South Western Railway and another on the Reading-Reigate line at Blackwater in 1849. Unfortunately funds ran out in 1866 and it was not until 1873 that the railway was finished by the London & South Western Railway. Despite the failure to get a railway up and running as soon as they had hoped, Knight and Spring continued with their development of the south of the town. In the 1860s they laid out Park Road south of the end at Frimley Road and crossing Crawley Hill to reach the Portsmouth Road at its eastern end. The new High Street was extended south to meet Park Road.

The Cambridge Hotel

One of Captain Knight's first moves when he purchased land near the London road in 1860 was to develop a hotel on the London Road near the entrance to the new Staff College at the Royal Military College. At the time this was on the corner of a muddy farm track which was later to become the High Street. The hotel, which went up in 1862 was named the 'Duke of Cambridge' after the then Commander-in-Chief of the Army. The area around the hotel, including the modern High Street, was called Cambridge Town. This also distinguished it from Yorktown further down the London Road near the entrance to the Old College.

THE CAMBRIDGE HOTEL AND LONDON ROAD
1927 79601

LONDON ROAD 2004 C12715k (Hazelle Jackson)

CAMBERLEY 1907 57916

PARK ROAD 1928 80699

By 1864 the town was now growing fast enough to need a second National School, this time in Cambridge Town to accommodate the children of the growing population there. Meanwhile the increasing numbers at the National School in Yorktown also led to the construction of a new school, on a site near St Michael's church donated by the Royal Military College. The school cost £1,400 and the money was raised from public subscriptions, donations and a grant from the National Society.

Major Spring developed the area to the north and west of Park Street. Historically this was site of the New Farm and France Hill. A substantial house, 'Franzhill', with attractive views over the wooded hill became the home of Viscount Southwell (and later the Camberley Arts Centre). Near the entrance to Franzhill Park on the Frimley Road was a smithy which served the local horses kept by the substantial homeowners, and an inn called 'The Four Horseshoes'. Nearby Major Spring built his own house, 'Franzhill Villa' later called 'The Whin'.

Other businessmen were also attracted by the location but not all were as successful as Captain Knight and Major Spring. A successful Swiss industrialist, Mr. Augustus Mongredien, bought 300 acres of rough wasteland off The Maultway in the early 1860s to start a silkworm farm. However the cold wind off Chobham Ridge proved unconducive to breeding silkworms, the manager he employed was inefficient (Mr Mongredien himself lived in London) and the farm failed. A second venture, to set up a plant and tree nursery in what is today Heatherside, also failed and Mr Mongredien is said to have made and lost at least three fortunes in the course of his life.

In the course of his doomed nursery venture Mr Mongredien planted many trees and laid out lawns and gardens, including Wellingtonia trees, which today line Longlands Way on the Heatherside Estate. The Company was named 'The Heatherside Nursery Company' until its failure in 1875 when the landowner Sir Gabriel foreclosed on the mortgage. Sir Gabriel turned the central area of the nursery into a farm which he rented to the Stokes family who established a dairy and went on to become the local milk suppliers to the town and surrounding area. Mongredien left behind a legacy in many fine specimens of trees and shrubs which can be found on the estate today.

LONDON ROAD 1901 46820

LONDON ROAD 1909 61463x

HIGH STREET 1919 68800p

HIGH STREET 1901 46832

TEKELS AVENUE 1931 83853

By the 1860s James Laurell's first fir plantations in Colling Wood, were ready for felling. This freed up more land for development and in 1862 two hundred acres of Cart Bottom were sold to the Royal Albert Orphanage Trust in memory of the Prince Consort, with funds raised by public subscription. The orphanage, which was completed in 1864, offered an education and training to sponsored orphans. At the end of World War Two the orphanage amalgamated with the Royal Alexandria School at Gatton in Surrey and the buildings were sold to the MOD who set up the Women's Royal Army Corps cadet training centre there. The last building to survive was the chapel which burnt down in 1987.

In 1869 Captain Knight, whose wife was French, sold Tekell's Castle and 330 acres to General Knight and moved to Bath. This did not sever his connection with Camberley as he retained his local business interests and continued to develop his land holdings in the area.

By the mid 1870s the first large houses in London Road had gone up, near the Cambridge Hotel. A substantial house, 'Heathfield House', was built in Knoll Road (where the Surrey Heath council offices now stand). Not far away 'The Knoll' was built, near the Obelisk, where Camberley Library now stands. This was a notoriously marshy area, there was a small pond in front of where the Library is now, and this may have been

BRACKENDALE 1908 61032

another reason for the construction of the Obelisk in the 18th century, with a light on its summit it may have warned night-time hunters of the low lying marshland below the hill. In 1875 the Rev Cox, who owned 'Knoll House' (later St Tarcisius School) grazed his cattle on the surrounding marshy fields.

The sprawling pinewoods and open heath which surrounded the town made the area a popular camping ground for Romany gypsies in the nineteenth century and into the early 1950s when they would travel down the A30 and A325 in colourful horse drawn caravans, and camp near the Blackwater river selling clothes pegs and home made baskets to the villagers.

As Cambridge Town grew, its name became a nuisance with the post often going astray to Cambridge in Cambridgeshire and the new town's name was changed to Camberley on the 15th January 1877. It is made up of three elements: 'Cam' which was a small stream which still flows under the Town Centre, 'Ber' from Amber Hill depicted on some old maps of the area, and 'Ley' which is a local suffix meaning pastureland or shelter.

During the 19th and 20th centuries Camberley was to extend right along the London road to Blackwater from here and eventually absorb Yorktown. The growth in the population in Camberley increased the local demand for services and a small row of single storey cottages near the Staff College entrance was converted into shops. The occupants included a solicitor, an architect, a butcher, a haberdasher's and a hardware store, Pank's, fondly remembered for many

years by older residents as being crammed to the rafters with every conceivable kind of kitchen utensil.

In the 1870s a number of medium sized houses were built in the France Hill area and many were rented out to officers studying at Sandhurst as there was no military housing provided by the army at the time. Further east a house called Collingwood Park stood in substantial grounds on Cart Bottom near the Maultway. Thomas Boys, a prosperous wine merchant from London with many business interests purchased this to develop upmarket housing locally. In 1881 Captain Knight sold a number of parcels of land on the western side of the Maultway for development, including a 15-acre plot where a substantial house called Graitney was built in the 1890s for Vice-Admiral Johnstone.

From 1896-8 Vice-Admiral Johnstone rented Graitney to the Crown Prince of Siam who was training as an office cadet at Sandhurst. (The house was later replaced by rawley Middle School.) Subsequently the Prince rented Frimley Park Manor House for a time. Royal protocol dictated that Royalty must sleep above staff and commoners so the Prince occupied the top room, a small room on the top floor of the house. A small step was added to the doorway of his room to ensure this was the case. It is still there today.

In 1885 as the demand for local shops increased, more houses were converted into shops, this time on the western side of the High Street, which started to develop as a shopping centre for the residents. Walter

LONDON ROAD 1909 61462x

Drake's livery stables and corn merchant's was established around this time. A short way down the High Street on the corner with Obelisk Street, Mr Craig of Barossa Farm ran a nursery garden and built a Georgian style house on the site set back from the road.

Much of the architecture in the commercial district of Camberley in the late nineteenth and early twentieth century bears the distinctive style of local architects H R and Poulter. A surviving example is the offices of Chancellors Estate Agents in the High Street.

In the closing years of the nineteenth century a Territorial Army drill hall was built next to the National School at the old Cambridge Town end on the north side of the London road and this was used for social gatherings by the local community for many years.

The Railway

The short-lived Sunningdale and Cambridge Town Railway Company was formed in 1863 and a route planned, starting from the Frimley Road and following the (now underground) bed of the Cam stream via Colling Ridge to Bagshot. In 1864 an Act of Parliament was obtained to pave the way and the first turf was cut followed by a celebratory dinner at the Cambridge Hotel. It was to be premature. Funds ran out and work was abandoned in 1866.

The railway finally arrived in 1873 - when the London & South Western completed the earlier track laid by the Sunningdale and Cambridge Town Railway and extended the route south from York Town to Frimley Green and Ash Vale and then on to Ascot in 1879.

THE STATION 1908 61031

FRIMLEY, THE RAILWAY ARMS 2004 F50701k (Hazelle Jackson)

After the railway arrived, the traffic on the turnpike road collapsed. In 1878 the Bedfont-Bagshot turnpike company was wound up.

Turnpike charges had always been greatly resented by local populations and in Camberley the residents lit a bonfire and roasted an ox in Laundry mead to celebrate its closure (near the modern Tesco supermarket at Blackwater). In 1888 Surrey Country Council took over responsibility for maintenance of the roads in the county.

The arrival of the railway had had a dramatic effect on the size of the town and encouraged more potential residents to travel out and review the new houses and facilities. By now the demand for houses and shopping was growing rapidly. In 1894 Camberley had a population of around 6,000, this was set to increase to 13,000 by 1914.

At the end of the 19th century Camberley was a settled and growing town.

CAMBERLEY ORDNANCE SURVEY MAP c1910

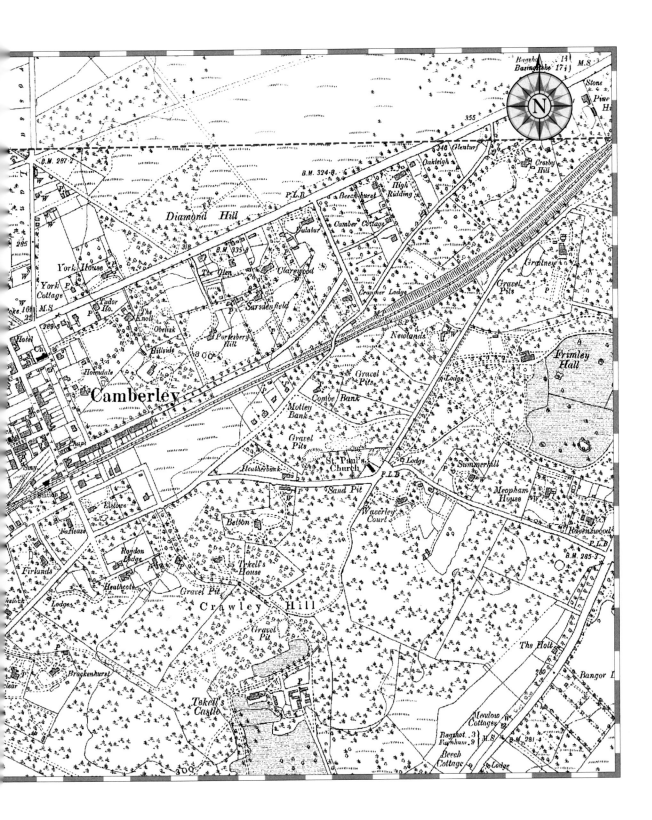

CHAPTER FOUR

Growth of Modern Camberley

THE HEATHLAND around Camberley remained largely barren and isolated on its windswept moors until the second half of the 20th century, when changes in agriculture, living styles and industrialisation, together with the decimation of the rabbit population by myxomatosis allowed the scrub to become rampant and weed trees to take a hold. This is the reason for much of the woodland in the area today.

Pine trees were believed to be medically beneficial and the air locally was regarded by doctors as particularly suited to invalids with chest complaints. Brompton Sanatorium

Did you know?
The Cinema

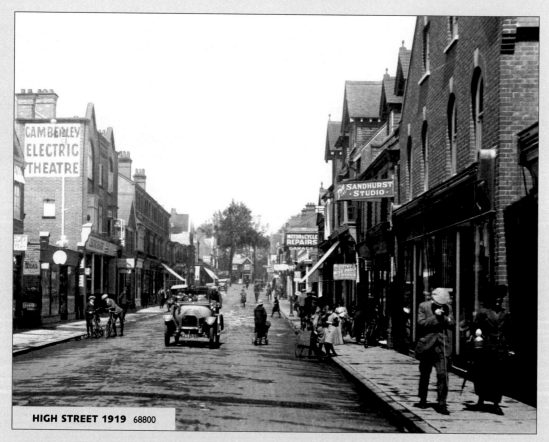

HIGH STREET 1919 68800

Camberley's first cinema, the Electric Theatre, opened in the High Street in 1910.

HIGH STREET 1925 78125

on the Old Bisley Road, was built for TB sufferers as a healthy location in the middle of pine forests in which to recuperate. It was opened by the Prince and Princess of Wales in 1904 and the Princess planted a Wellingtonia to mark the occasion. The building is now the Ridgewood Centre.

The wealthier residents of early Camberley were very involved in philanthropic work. In June 1916 Princess Alexandra visited Camberley and had lunch with Mr and Mrs Francis Brenton at 'Ravenswood'. Boys from the Royal Albert Orphan Asylum were the guard of honour. She also visited 'Conewood' which was a holiday crèche for London children under five.

By 1900 Mr Craig's house on the corner of Obelisk Street had become 'Lords House',

a boarding house for young gentlemen attending Colonel Fox's 'crammer' in Knoll Road as they tried to get into the RMC. Mrs Mortimer's School for Dancing was also set up around this time locally and was later to achieve worldwide fame as the Elmhurst Ballet School. (In 2004 the Elmhurst school left the area and relocated in Birmingham).

Around 1900 a local draper James Page set up shop in the High Street with ambitions to expand. In 1910 he was able to purchase Lord's House and added shop fronts to it founding the famous local drapers, Page's of Camberley. Page's store was eventually absorbed by Allders department store who occupy the site today.

Other businesses were moving into the area which was growing rapidly. In 1909

HIGH STREET 1936 87778A

Percy Wellard, a lady's hairdresser at Harrods was recommended that the area was a promising location for a new business by one of his customers there. Wellard visited the burgeoning town, liked what he saw and took a High Street shop near Page's in 1909.

In his memoirs Gordon Wellard, Percy's son, who took over the business in 1947, recalled how 50% of early hairdressing was Marcel Waving and the other 50% making and fitting hairpieces for the elaborate female hairstyles of the time. As electricity did not

The Tracco

Aldershot's first buses were operated by the Aldershot & Farnborough Motor Omnibus Company Ltd in 1906. In 1912 this was reconstituted as a new company called the Aldershot & District Traction Co, universally known on the Hampshire Surrey Borders as The Tracco. Up to the Second World War it rapidly expanded its service in and ran regular buses between Aldershot, Farnborough and Camberley. In 1969 the Government formed the National Bus Company and the end was in sight for the traditional green and cream of the Aldershot Company. In 1972 the 'Tracco' merged with neighbouring company Thames Valley to form AlderValley.

come to Camberley as a whole until 1922 his father had to heat up his curling tongs with a generator. As the only hairdresser for 15 miles he also spent a lot of time cycling round to his remoter clients.

Mr Percy Wellard may have had a bicycle; other working people in the area took the bus as well. Some of first buses to serve the area were run by 'The Tracco', Aldershot and District Traction Company whose green and yellow livery became a familiar site for the next 60 years.

THE CAMBRIDGE HOTEL AND LONDON ROAD 1927 79601

The Urban District of Frimley was formed in 1894. In 1906 the council built new offices on land it had acquired on the London road, on a site known as Tough's Nursery, formerly part of the Franzhill estate In 1898 some old cottages on the London Road opposite the Duke of Cambridge, were converted into shops. One of these was later given a mock Tudor frontage and was to become a familiar site to visitors to the town as Betty Brown's Tea Shop, with a painted wooden figure of a lady at the entrance.

FRIMLEY ROAD, AT THE JUNCTION WITH LONDON ROAD 1931   83848X

Did you know?

Teashops

Betty Brown's and the Mandarin were the only tea shops which the officer cadets were allowed to visit in the town. Many local romances flourished over the teacups.

BETTY BROWN'S TEASHOP ZZZ01307

LONDON ROAD, THE DUKE OF YORK HOTEL 1931 83847

Recreation Ground

The London Road Recreation Ground was established alongside the new council buildings in 1906. The neighbouring site went up for sale in 1908. It was bought by a consortium of local businessmen, which included Mr. Pank, of Pank's Hardware Emporium.

Recreation Ground Gardens 1931 83858

LONDON ROAD 1936 87781

Note the Furrier's Shop.

Camberley itself remained a military university town for the first half of the 20th century. Until the 1950s many of the smartest shops in the area were to be found in the North Camp area between Farnborough and the main military garrison a few miles south of Camberley.

Franzhill House and surrounding land was bought by Mrs Forbes who renamed it France Hill - quite probably because a German sounding name was not felt to be a good idea in the years leading up to the First World War. Building also continued along the Frimley Road and by 1913 Frimley was enjoying a mini boom of its own.

In 1912-13 Camberley Heath golf club was set up with a course on a long strip of land to the south east of the town. This was land typical of the area before tree planting: heather, gorse, bracken and clumps of pine. It had a very aristocratic membership including Prince Christian of Schleswig-Holstein who was married to Helena August Victoria, Queen Victoria's daughter. Prince Christian had the honour of hitting the first ball. By March of that same year it was announced that there were 528 members, including ladies.

In the first half of the 20th century, much of local upper class life in Camberley centred around the golf club. Female caddies were employed from 1915 but women and 'tradesmen' were expected to know their place. (Until the 1930s, tradesmen could not be members and the Artisan membership class of the 1930s were only invited to become full members in 1946 following a crisis in the club's finances). Later the tennis courts, bowling green and woodland were sold for development to secure the club's future and a new clubhouse was built in 1990.

But the skies were darkening and in 1914 war broke out with Germany. At first everyone thought it would be over quickly but as time went on many of the women whose husbands were away fighting found that money was very short. In her memoirs, in 1982, Chrissie Jebbitt recalled how: 'as the weary years dragged on, my poor mum found it hard to feed us all. She tried hard to make her money go round. But it was not enough by a long way. The ladies of the churches organised local wives and mothers to start making shirts for our soldiers at the front. And they had to be made absolutely perfect, for the sum of 9½d. I remember well my mum taking the babies' pram and loading it up with as many as she thought she could make in a week. She often stayed up half the night, to get them done in time to get the money for them and get another lot on Thursdays at the Drill Hall. My eldest sister Nan and me used to help her sew on the name tags. We used to put little messages on the back of the paper to the soldiers who received the shirts'.

Chrissie herself, like many working class young women locally, found employment in service with a local family: 'I would have loved to have trained as a nurse, but at 14 I was too young. I had to go to a big house and learn how to do work properly. I had to sleep at this place and was only allowed to go home one half day a week, and every other Sunday. I was very lonely and miserable and the other girls who worked there were all so much older than I was. They paid me £1 a month, and my food. I had to get up at 6.30am and often did not go to bed till 11pm.'

LONDON ROAD 1925 78123

The heavy losses among young men in the First World War affected the local community, like so many others in the UK, and the loss of one particular young man was to have a significant impact on the next stage of development of the town. Before the First World War Squire Hollins was a major local landowner living at Watchett's House, between Frimley and Camberley. His son and heir who was expected to inherit the family estate was killed in the First World War. When Squire Hollins died in 1922 his daughter Hildegarde inherited the estate. She sold the Watchett's and Bristow estates to local businessman Nicholas Verran in 1924. (Watchett's House was sold to another successful local business owner, Mr Over).

The Verrans had arrived from Cornwall in 1897 and rapidly established a flourishing meat and fish business in the town. In 1929 Nicholas Verran put up part of the Watchett's estate for sale and this led to further housing development locally. Verran, like Thomas Boys in the 19th century, wanted to develop good quality housing and placed a number of restrictions on the size and type of development permitted, to ensure this. He is commemorated today in Upper Verran Road.

In 1929 the Urban District of Frimley became Frimley and Camberley Urban District Council, a change which reflected the growing importance of Camberley in the local pecking order. In 1929 a plot on the Watchett's site was purchased for Frimley and Camberley County school which opened on the Frimley Road in 1931 with 40 pupils.

FRIMLEY STREET c1955 F50054

Frimley Park Manor House

THE HOUSE, FRIMLEY PARK c1955 F50039

Frimley Park Manor House had a series of owners in the 20th century. Between the World Wars in the twentieth century it was owned by Theodore Ralli, a cotton merchant from Liverpool, who made many improvements including landscaping the grounds and installing paneling brought from Chillingham Castle. During the Second World War, the house became a maternity hospital, and from 1947 to 1950 the Officers' Association used the house. In 1951 the house and grounds were taken over by the War Department for the WRAC Staff College, which remained until 1957.

In 1957, the Amery Committee proposed that a training centre for the CCF and ACF be established, under a Board of Governors and the War Office selected Frimley Park Manor House for this function. It was opened as the Cadet Training Centre in 1959. During the more than forty years since opening, over 90,000 adults and cadets have passed through CTC. In 2004 the historic gardens were restored to their original design.

In the 1930s the newly growing hobby of photography had its adherents and the largest and most influential camera club in the area was Windlesham Camera Club which was founded in 1935 by John Hayward and soon had over 300 members. This too enjoyed royal patronage as the village was not far from Bagshot Park, where members of the Royal Family lived on the edge of the Windsor estate and Princess Elizabeth was a keen photographer. In its first year members filmed a 'Windlesham Tribute' in memory of the 1935 Coronation. This film was shown at Bagshot Park to HRH The Duke of Connaught, who had become Patron of the club, and Lady Patricia Ramsay. John Hayward organised an active social programme and the club's first Annual Exhibition, opened by the Hon. Anthony Asquith attracted over 500 entries from camera artists as far apart as New York and Budapest. Although it closed down during the war, the club re-opened in 1948 and HRH Princess Elizabeth, became Patron and opened the International Exhibition in Camberley in 1949. Its name was changed to the Camberley and Windlesham Camera Club to reflect its reach and today it continues to be a friendly and active club for all enthusiastic photographers.

After the Second World War a new sports club arrived on the scene which quickly made its presence felt. The Camberley Cricket Club was started in 1944 by Col H M Marshall-Harris. In 1946 members entertained a Surrey Colts team which included the young Eric Bedser and Tony Lock, watched by the King of the Hellenes. In 1947 the club leased a site on the Watchett's estate which was later conveyed to them by the owner Mr W B Verran in 1950. The cricket square was laid out by Messrs Gaze of Kingston and the ground was formally opened on 22 June 1952 by the New Zealand High Commissioner.

Did you know?

POW Camp

German POWs were held in a large tented camp at Frith Hill in the Frimley Fuel Allotments area. During the Second World War a large tented camp was erected there to house up to 10,000 Prisoners of War. They were brought by train to Frimley station and then marched up to the camp at Frith Hill. Many trees were felled to make space for the camp and this also preserved the local heathland there.

POW'S MARCHING TO FRITH HILL ZZZ01309

Over the years the club hosted many overseas teams and some notable benefits including those for Alec Bedser in 1953 and Jim Laker in 1956. The first pavilion was built by members in 1951 at a cost of £100. In 1971 they sold land to pay for a new one which was professionally built this time and cost £10,000. The new facilities obviously did the trick because the club won the inaugural year of the Surrey County League in 1972. The club continued to prosper during the century and in 1994 David Gower (England international and former captain) was elected vice President. In 1997 the club sold woodland at the end of the ground to finance a new pavilion which cost £650,000 - a far cry from the £100 spent in 1951. It was opened in 1998 by international cricketer Shaun Udal.

After the Second World War there was considerable pressure on country areas around London to accommodate the thousands of Londoners who had lost their homes in the war. The restrictions on development imposed by so much land held by the Army limited how far Camberley could help with overspill estates and a lot of attention was diverted to Bracknell and Basingstoke as a result. However after some negotiation the Council settled on Old Dean Common where a council estate was built on 94 acres to the east of Caesar's Camp.

FRIMLEY ROAD c1965 C12126

HIGH STREET c1965 C12085p

Not only houses but also jobs were needed for the new residents. Up to the Second World War Camberley was a fairly self-contained place and while there was full employment, there was not much surplus employment. Before and after the war a lot of industrial development took place around the Farnborough to the south where new light industries had sprung up to service the Royal Aircraft Establishment.

However some industrial development also took place on the former peat moorland between Frimley and the London Road at the Western end of Camberley and this increased rapidly after the motorway arrived in 1973.

In the 1960s local councillors were firmly of the opinion that an expanding town needed a new shopping centre and the entire area between the High Street and Park Street was flattened to make way for a new shopping developed by the Arndale group. Keeping the large houses in the area going became a struggle for many owners in the 1960s. Some of the larger houses were sold for schools - Graitney for example was sold by its owner James Cubitt, the architect, to the Country Council and in 1969 became Crawley Ridge Preparatory School. Others had their grounds split up for more intensive development.

After 1966, the remaining Frimley Park estate was much reduced in size. Firstly by the widening of the Frimley Road to the south of the park into a dual carriageway, secondly by the building of Frimley Park Hospital and lastly by the building of the Gilbert Road housing estate between the park and the M3. In 1989, a further encroachment of 2.7 acres was made by the hospital.

Local arts and music facilities were also enjoyed popular support. Camberley theatre was built next to the library in Knoll road in 1966 with seating for 400 and a studio and conference space. At the other end of town the Agincourt Ballroom catered to fans of rock music.

THE AGINCOURT BALLROOM, LONDON ROAD 2004 C12717k (Hazelle Jackson)

At the Yorktown end of Camberley is the Agincourt Ballroom, popularly known as 'The Adj'. 'The Adj' supplied a young audience with stars such as The Who, Cream and Pink Floyd in the 1960s alongside lesser but perennially popular local acts like Johnny Kidd and the Pirates and Screaming Lord Sutch. Live shows are still held there today from time to time.

A noted local businessman who made his name starting out as a pop promoter in the area in the 1960s was Bob Potter, now best known as the multi-millionaire owner of

THE LAKESIDE COUNTRY CLUB 2004 C12716k (Hazelle Jackson)

the Lakeside Country Club at Frimley. In the 1960s Potter was a member of a local band and also owned a music shop. Branching out as a band manager he used to arrange local gigs for the likes of the Beatles and the Rolling Stones.

'We used to pay the Fab Four £45-a-night and the Stones got £65 - they were both crazy bands but they were also very nice people'. The author remembers slipping Bob £23 in an envelope back in the early 1960s in payment for the band at a youth club dance in a church hall in North Camp. His enduring passion however proved to be darts and in 2004 Lakeside had been playing host to the World Darts Championships for nearly 20 years with Potter as its enthusiastic patron.

Another millionaire businessman from Camberley has a rather more unexpected connection with the local music scene. Charles Church, who with his wife founded the eponymous house builders in 1965, went to school in Windlesham near Camberley. The group's southern headquarters today are in Knoll Road, Camberley and the company sponsors the Charles Church Camberley Brass Band.

In 1971 Surrey County Council reorganised local secondary education and Collingwood College was created from a merger of Camberley Grammar School, Barossa Secondary School and Bagshot Secondary School. In September 1994 it became a self-governing Technology College and, after consultation with parents, the Governing Body adopted Foundation Status under the new Schools' Framework which came into effect on 1st September 1999. The College is based at the edge of the old Frimley Park estate near the A325.

The area received a major boost to its growth with the announcement in the 1960s of the decision to build the M3 motorway through the area. The eventual route it took when it opened in 1973 was across the industrial area between Frimley and Camberley, across the southern end of Frimley Park, through the Collingwood estate and across the former grounds of the Royal Albert Orphanage, by then used by the Women's Royal Army College as a staff college.

The arrival of the motorway also brought renewed interest in the town as a location for new offices and many new office buildings were built, in the hinterland south of the London Road and along the Frimley road near the Blackwater river. Many of these were light industrial, high-tec service industries moving into Camberley for the first time.

The growth of the area also brought new changes to the structure of local government in the area. In 1974 the Borough of Surrey Heath was incorporated after the merger of Frimley and Camberley Urban District Council with Bagshot Rural District Council.

The M3 motorway had divided the former Royal Albert Orphanage site into two and when the WRAC Officers Training school moved into the RMAS in the 1980s it was

FRIMLEY, HIGH STREET 2004 F50703k (Hazelle Jackson)

FRIMLEY, HIGH STREET 1921 69919

inevitable that it should be the next site to be developed. The site was eventually developed as a large private housing estate in 1987. By 1987 building land in Camberley was £1m an acre. Gradually the spacious grounds around the middle class 'quality' homes of the nineteenth and early twentieth century filled up with new housing. Only the Army's substantial holdings remained relatively safe from the attentions of developers.

As the need to collect fuel on the Allotments diminished, the Army used the land for exercises and local people used it for recreation. Inevitably the prospect of alternative, more 'profitable' uses began to be canvassed; an extended and bitterly fought planning battle took place in the 1980s following a proposal to convert some of the land in the remaining Frimley Fuel Allotments, into a golf course. Opponents said the land should be retained for the public as originally intended. Some of the golf course supporters pointed out that at least by having a golf course on the land, it was being retained as open space and less likely to come under renewed pressure from developers. The golf course eventually opened in 1990 and among the charities which have benefited from Frimley Fuel Allotments funding are Frimley Hospital, Watchetts, Camberley and Frimley Recreation ground. Around 100 acres of heath and wood remain open to local people.

The Basingstoke canal had ceased to be a viable commercial property early in the 20th century and had a chequered career up to the Second World War. Following an incident in 1957, when troops returning from an evening training exercise blew up Lock XXII at Frimley, the pound drained and it deteriorated rapidly. In 1968, following severe flooding a concrete dam was installed to prevent water flooding out over Ash Embankment and this dried up the upper stretches and it declined still further. But its supporters never gave up and after many further setbacks London's Lost Route to Basingstoke was finally restored. It was officially opened again as a waterway by the Duke of Kent on 10th May 1991.

In 1949 the last commercial traffic to use the Basingstoke canal took a load of timber to Spanton's Yard at Monument Bridge, Woking. In the 1980s it was finally purchased by Surrey and Hampshire County Councils. The two councils formed the Basingstoke Canal Authority and over the years, with lots of help from the Canal Society, volunteers and numerous organisations, they managed to bring the canal back to life. Materials were often provided by the councils, this included oak from nearby woods which was used to rebuild lock gates. In 1991 after expenditure of £4 million the Basingstoke Canal was fully restored through 32 miles from the River Wey to Greywell Tunnel.

FRIMLEY, THE WHARF, A LOCK KEEPER'S COTTAGE 2004 F50702k (Hazelle Jackson)

A further major refurbishment of Camberley town centre was carried out in the early 1990s when Main Square shopping mall was completed. The radical transformation was completely financed by private developers and the refurbishment of Main Square was one of the private sector's largest financial investments in the Borough. The mall was designed by local architects Lyons Seaman Hoar with shops and architecture designed to create 'an elegant Victorian atmosphere'.

HIGH STREET AND MAIN SQUARE ENTRANCE 2004 C12714k (Hazelle Jackson)

HIGH STREET 2004 C12718k (Hazelle Jackson)

LONDON ROAD c1955 C12104

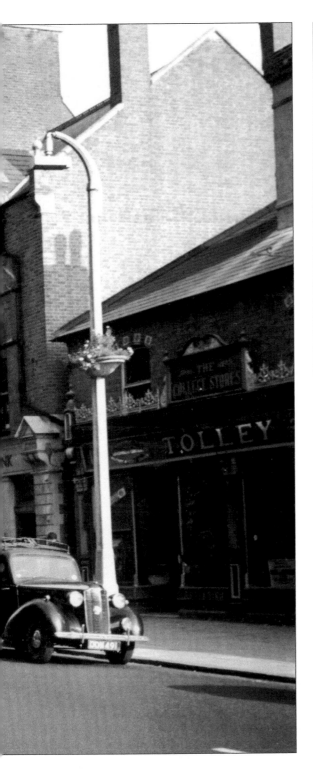

BUS TIMETABLE ZZZ01308

Further west The Meadows, a £32m open-air retail park, developed by Tesco and Marks and Spencer, opened on former farmland on the county boundary with Hampshire and Berkshire near Blackwater in the 1990s.

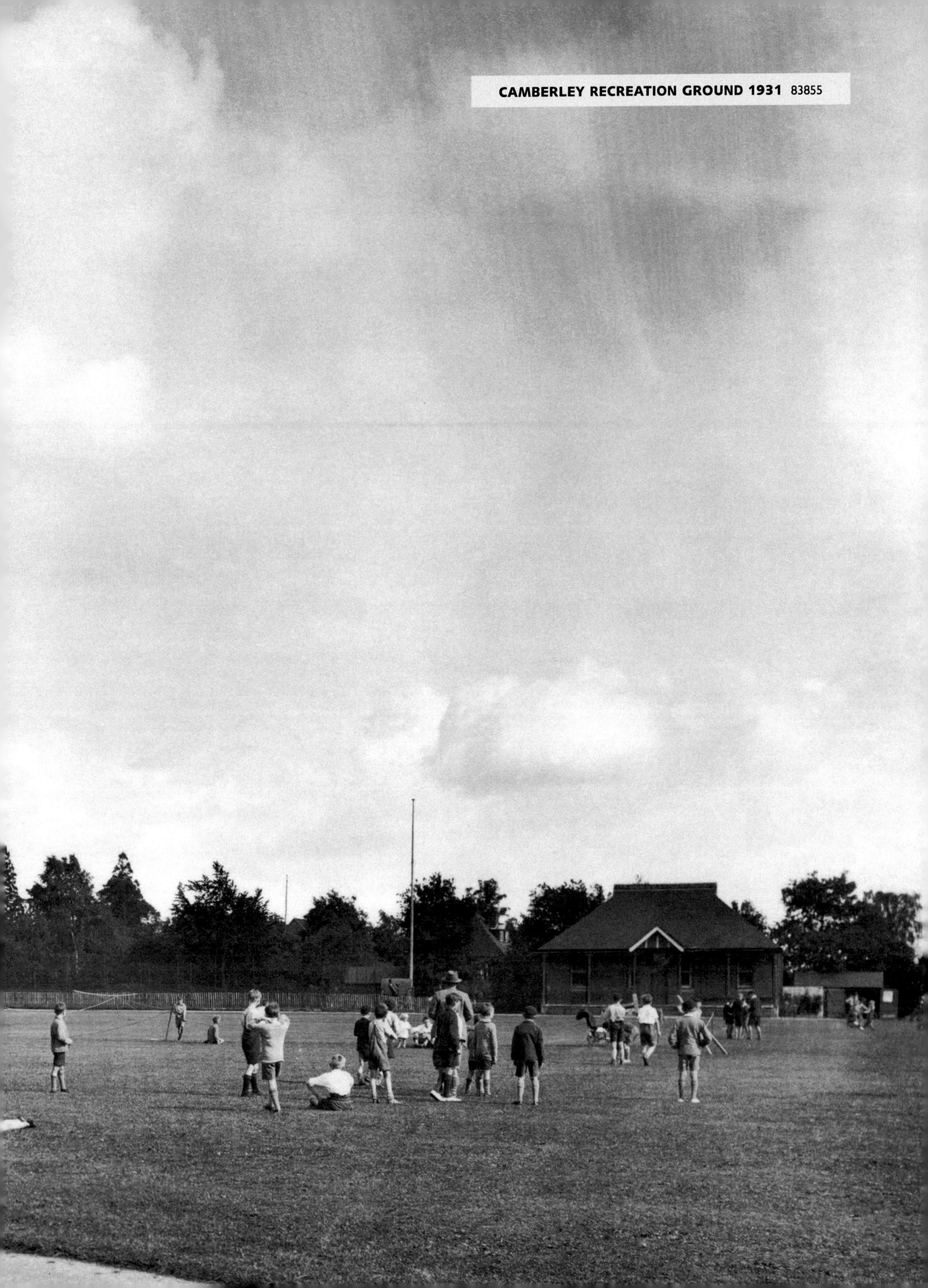

CAMBERLEY RECREATION GROUND 1931 83855

CHAPTER FIVE

Camberley Today

BY THE start of the New Millennium in 2000, Surrey Heath was one of the most prosperous areas in the south-east with 84,000 residents, a remarkably rapid growth in less than two hundred years. Among the celebrations held to mark the event was a three day 'Celebration in the Parks' weekend at Frimley Lodge Park including historical re-enactments of the history of the area. When Camberley Park, the area behind the Council offices, was opened in Millennium Year, the 18th century Obelisk tower was made accessible to the general public once more.

Camberley today is full of surprises. Driving out to Camberley along the A30 from London can be a disconcerting experience for anyone, who, like the author, grew up in the area in the 1950s and 60s.

AMERICAN GOLF DISCOUNT STORE 2004 C12719k (Hazelle Jackson)

After passing through Bagshot the motorist begins the familiar ascent to the Jolly Farmer roundabout where the A30 meets the A325. Here in 2004 a shock awaits. Where once a venerable inn greeted generations of travellers, today a bold white building comes into view emblazoned with the stars and stripes topped by a bold new sign: 'American Golf Discount Centre'. The old inn now caters to the golfing needs of owners of the shiny 4 x4s parked in its car park. The original building is still there somewhere under the new paint and golf putters but the ghosts of the highwaymen who once frequented it are now a faint memory. Its previous use, as the Mongolian Barbecue was perhaps more appropriate!

In the town centre visitors to Surrey Heath

TOWN HALL 2004 C12721k (Hazelle Jackson)

Council Offices in Knoll Road find themselves confronted with the ugly offspring of a modern block of redbrick flats and a dull 3* East European-style holiday hotel. The mediocrity of the building is redeemed by the Surrey Heath museum which is on the premises and holds regular and attractive displays of the town's history. Behind the Council offices a new housing development has ascended the hill and surrounded the Obelisk.

Did you know?

Panto

The 2003/4 pantomine, 'Cinderella' at the Camberley Theatre, broke box office records with a total audience of over 15,000 people.

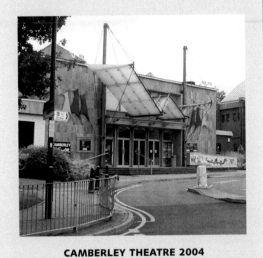

CAMBERLEY THEATRE 2004
C12728k (Hazelle Jackson)

Camberley Theatre at the end of Knoll Road, with its jaunty nautical façade, is enthusiastically supported by the local community although it has struggled to balance the books due to its small size. In 2003/4 the pantomime 'Cinderella' broke Box Office records with attendances of 15,000 beating 'Peter Pan's' previous record and exceeding 10,000 for the first time ever for a panto at the Camberley Theatre. From time to time a banner strung across the middle of the High Street, announces a new production at the theatre and in Spring 2004 it was the

Gilbert and Sullivan operetta 'The Pirates of Penzance' in a neat tribute to Sir Arthur Sullivan one of Camberley's most famous sons.

Travelling west along the A30, the Cambridge hotel still occupies its corner site at the top of the High Street, now rebranded as 'The Cambridge' and with its lower storey painted a garish bright blue and yellow. Some Victorian shops have survived on the eastern side of the High Street but the western side has been given over to modern developments including a dated façade for Allders' department store department (due for a facelift soon). The entrances to the Main Square shopping mail are also on the western side of the street.

THE CAMBRIDGE 2004 C12722k (Hazelle Jackson)

The Old Thai House

One of the most popular Asian restaurants is the Old Thai House on the London Road near its junction with the High Street, in the former Betty Brown's tearooms. After it ceased to be Betty Brown's tearooms, probably in the 1960s, the teashop had a troubled history. It was rescued in the 1990s by Preeya Buddery and her family who converted it into the Old Thai House restaurant and imported antique panelling from her family home in Thailand to replace that removed by previous owners. Mrs Buddery was anxious to dispel any bad spirits which had come to reside there in earlier years so she consulted a Buddhist priest. Acting on his advice she imported spirit doors from Thailand to allow trapped spirits to come and go freely and the business has prospered ever since. The doors can be seen on the upper floor of the restaurant.

Old Thai House

THE OLD THAI HOUSE 2004 C12701k (Hazelle Jackson)

Traffic jams are common on the A30 and bus lanes, by central government dictat, are being installed on the London Road to persuade the reluctant residents to leave their cars at home and take to public transport. These have not had an enthusiastic welcome in Camberley. Despite considerable government pressure to take to the buses, residents here are sticking resolutely to their cars: Camberley has one of the highest percentages of car ownership in the south east of England. No doubt they need them to carry their golf clubs.

On the south side of the London Road is the empty site next to Park Street, to the west of the Main Square shopping mall, vacant for several years prior to 2004 after several attempts to get a development off the ground failed.

Finally in Spring 2004 developers Crest Nicholson were chosen by Surrey Heath Council, from over 18 other bidders, to develop the site; even then it was a close vote on the Council with some members expressing misgivings about the terms agreed with the developers. With a deal agreed CN submitted a planning application for a £100 million scheme for the site and in early July 2004 the new scheme, designed by DLG Architects, went on display for public comment.

Crest Nicholson's plans for the seven-acre site include new shops, a leisure complex and flats in a landscaped parkland setting. At the heart of the development they proposed to built a 128,000 sq ft 'leisure box' with a nine screen cinema, a 20 lane bowling alley, health & fitness unit, restaurants, cafes and a climbing wall, all accessed from a three storey glazed atrium. There will also be 120,000 sq ft of new shops, facing on to Park Street, connecting with Main Square. On the edge of the development will be 163 private flats plus 55 'affordable' flats (a relative term in Camberley) designed to integrate with the area.

Councillor Keith Bush, portfolio holder responsible for the town centre, said: 'The majority of local residents have been hugely supportive of the proposed redevelopment plans and now that we have an application we welcome their comments and ideas. This is an exciting time for the borough of Surrey Heath as we move into a new era for Camberley town centre.'

Continuing west down London Road, past the Staff pub, much of the old town to the south of the road, has been swept away by office blocks, built in the domineering post-modern style favoured by developers and town planners of the current generation. Many sites have been reduced to building plots with cranes raising their long necks to the skyline, where bold hoardings announce yet another cost-efficient, energy-efficient office building to lure the light-industrial, high-tech service industry on which much of the local economy now depends.

To the north of the London Road the old redbrick National School is now the Al-Kharafi Islamic Centre - testimony to the changing social structure of the modern town - while the Territorial Army occupies the former Drill Hall next door, once the scene of many social gatherings for townsfolk.

Occasionally an old building, like original 1906 Town Hall building survives but the relentless pressure from developers is clear here. The old Odeon Cinema, an Art Deco classic on London Road is now isolated between building sites, awaiting its fate.

The spire of St Michael's garrison church dominates the skyline on the northern side of the road on the approach to Yorktown opposite the Duke of York hotel on the corner of the Frimley Road.

The wooded grounds of Royal Military Academy Sandhurst line the northern side of the London Road overlooking Camberley but are fenced off with barbed wire and well guarded these days. In the first half of

The Regal Cinema

LONDON ROAD c1955 C12081

The Regal Cinema opened on the London road on the 27th August 1932 when the firms shown were Jack Hulbert and Cicely Courtnidge in 'Jack's The Boy' and Laurel and Hardy in 'One Good Turn'.

Over the century other cinemas in the town were pulled down to make way for new buildings as Camberley grew but the Regal survived, in its distinctive Art Deco style, mutating through several names changes – including becoming an Odeon as it changed hands. Now however the end is approaching and today the old cinema building, forlornly decked out as a snooker hall, defiantly waits the arrival of the bulldozers.

THE ODEON CINEMA 2004 C12702k (Hazelle Jackson)

the 20th century the grounds of the RMAS were open to local residents, who could walk there, appreciate the wildlife and even on occasion swim in the lakes. This facility was closed in the mid twentieth century for security reasons.

In June 2003, on an initiative by the Commandant Major-General Andrew Ritchie to integrate the Military Academy into the local community, the Army staged the RMAS Heritage Day at Sandhurst and opened its gates to the public. Local people were invited to explore the site and share in its history while raising money for charity. This was a great success with over 5,000 people present.

It was repeated in June 2004 when local residents could stroll in the grounds of the Academy, study the history preserved in the buildings, admire the lakes and appreciate the army's two hundred years of history on the site. Despite the generally poor weather the sun shone, and the rain clouds held off long enough for the band to play 'Beating the Retreat' before the downpour arrived.

On 9-10 July 2004 the RMAS hosted 'Music on Fire' in the grounds to celebrate 60 years of the Army Benevolent Fund. This was a musical and firework extravaganza organised by Major Sir Michael Parker CBE, the man responsible for HM the Queen's Golden Jubilee Festival in 2002 and the Queen Mother's 100th birthday celebrations in 2000.

Most of the old shops at the Yorktown end of the London Road in Camberley have gone now. Vacant building lots and aggressive office blocks, many empty and seeking tenants, dominate this end of the town. A few local shops have hung on and the former Criterion Cinema is now a jauntily painted Asian supermarket.

ASIAN FOOD SHOP, LONDON ROAD 2004
C12720k (Hazelle Jackson)

Passing the Agincourt Ballroom and MacDonald's, the Trollope and Colls' concrete elephant survives, now painted white and mounted on a plinth alongside the London road. This has long been a familiar sign to drivers heading west, since the 1960s.

The Crown

The Crown pub, now stranded between empty office blocks, was put up for sale in 2004. There are stories that part of the building is the original miller's house from the 17th century. The frontage has two aspects with one possibly older than the other suggesting an extension in the 19th century but the 1802 Enclosure map in the local museum shows no building on the site. The only evidence for the claim is that an old millstone once formed the back step to the pub.

THE CROWN, LONDON ROAD 2004
C12712k (Hazelle Jackson)

The Blackwater roundabout is both an aesthetic and a practical disaster, a text book example of all that is wrong with modern planning. It looks awful and it doesn't work when it comes to moving the traffic. Choking traffic, bullying traffic lights, confusing lanes, multiple road junctions, building works and garish advertisements for yet more gargantuan office blocks in the future - this is a singularly unattractive area of Camberley.

Did you know?
Gilbert and Sullivan

Sir Arthur Sullivan, the Victorian composer of Gilbert and Sullivan fame, grew up in a cottage on the London road when his father was bandmaster at the Royal Military College in the nineteenth century. The family lived in a modest house – Albany Cottages, which once stood on the site now occupied by the Drive-Thru McDonalds on the London road. Hungry drivers now munch their burgers on the site where young Arthur Sullivan practised on the instruments in his father's band. There is a commemorative plaque on the wall outside, now rapidly being covered by encroaching plants.

SULLIVAN'S PLAQUE 2004
C12723k (Hazelle Jackson)

The Camberley Concrete Elephant.

In 1963 the artist and writer Barbara Jones was asked to design the London Lord Mayor's Show on the theme of building. Trollope and Colls were leading city builders and Jones designed an elephant for their float, which has survived to the present day. It was made, all but the ears, from standard concrete pipes and held a section of pipe between its trunk and tusks and was constructed at the firm's Camberley works.

It was driven up to London for the show. Afterwards it was put up over the front entrance to Trollope and Coll's Pipeworks near the Blackwater roundabout where for many years it has been a familiar landmark on the A30. It has survived the redevelopment of the area and still greets modern travellers on the A30 today.

THE CAMBERLEY CONCRETE ELEPHANT 2004
C12729k (Hazelle Jackson)

In July 2004 the former Lamb pub languished forlornly by the side of the roundabout, stripped of its fittings with a large demolition notice pinned on its front and awaiting the arrival of the bulldozers. On the northern edge of the roundabout, reached through a myriad traffic lanes and lights is The Meadows retail park developed in the 1990s by Tesco and Marks and Spencer. Nothing more needs to be said about this, the description 'Retail Park' conveys it all.

LONDON ROAD, BLACKWATER END 2004 C12727k (Hazelle Jackson)

WOODLAND TRACK IN SWINLEY FOREST 2004
C12726k (Hazelle Jackson)

MEETING OF THE BLACKWATER RIVER AND WISH 2004
C12724k (Hazelle Jackson)

The Blackwater river joins the Wish stream and the boundaries of three counties Surrey, Hampshire and Berkshire meet here channelled into a culvert near Tesco's car park.

As yet another empty office block is added to all the others along the London road, the stalled driver in the traffic jam muses on the eternal mysteries of modern life and accounting – what arcane calculations can render empty office blocks profitable and when did economics and aesthetics achieve so complete a divorce as in the present day? More to the point, what motivates planners to approve this uglification of our landscape? The Blackwater roundabout is an instructive example of all that is wrong with modern architecture and town planning if anyone is listening, which presumably they aren't.

Blackwater village over the bridge is rundown and shabby. The legendary motorcyclists' bikers' café where once Hell's Angels hung out and hundreds of bikers gathered nightly has long since gone. Next to the railway station flags flap in the winds above another empty office block in its landscaped park.

Only if you turn south here and drive out towards Hawley can you catch glimpses of the rural communities displaced by modern development.

Camberley has undergone many changes in recent years and the building boom of the last decade shows few signs of slowing down. Much of London Road is now dominated by large unsightly office blocks and the old rural character of the area has been swept away round the town centre. The M3 thundering past to the south has been a mixed blessing, bringing with it prosperity but also intrusive development. Traffic in the town centre is more congested than ever and in-fill housing has replaced the spacious villas of the past.

Hawley

The parish of Hawley is sited in the northeast corner of Hampshire and covers an area of 4,600 acres, stretching from Blackwater through part of Minley to Cove. There are many hundreds of acres of common land, with walks among heather, bracken and pine trees and along the Blackwater river valley.

Hawley Manor, once owned by John Norris who built the Obelisk in the eighteenth century, was refurbished and put up for sale in 2004 after lying vacant for many years. It is said it was once a hunting lodge for Oliver Cromwell. The original village school has survived although now much extended.

HAWLEY, THE VILLAGE 1906 57004

FRIMLEY BRIDGE 1906 55637

Yet thanks to the foresight of those early developers, who built large houses in landscaped grounds, and to the restrictions on development imposed by the Army's occupation of vast acres of heath land, Camberley still offers something of the same pine clad healthy area and attractive walks in its hinterland which first attracted the Victorians to the area. Their spirits linger on in the pine-clad hills today.

FRIMLEY LODGE PARK BROCHURE ZZZ01300

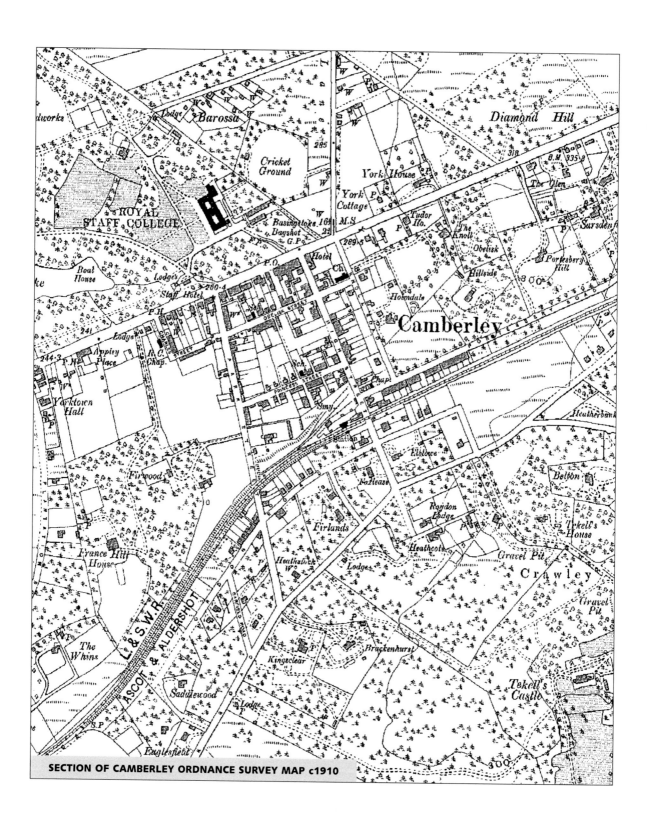

SECTION OF CAMBERLEY ORDNANCE SURVEY MAP c1910

ACKNOWLEDGEMENTS

Major Ken Molyneux-Carter (Rtd), Cadet Training Centre, Frimley.
Mary Bennett, Assistant Curator, Surrey Health Museum.
Mrs Preeya Buddery, Director, The Old Thai House Restaurant, Camberley.
Chairman and members of the Surrey and Hampshire Canal Society.
Ned and Gus Paul.

FURTHER READING

'The Story of Camberley 1798-1987' by Gordon Wellard. Self Published.
'A History of Bagshot and Windlesham' Marion Eadle, Phillimore 1977.

Francis Frith
Pioneer Victorian Photographer

Francis Frith, founder of the world-famous photographic archive, was a multi-talented man. A devout Quaker and a highly successful Victorian businessman, he was philosophical by nature and pioneering in outlook. By 1855 he had already established a wholesale grocery business in Liverpool, and sold it for the astonishing sum of £200,000, which is the equivalent today of over £15,000,000. Now in his thirties, and captivated by the new science of photography, Frith set out on a series of pioneering journeys up the Nile and to the Near East.

He was the first photographer to venture beyond the sixth cataract of the Nile. Africa was still the mysterious 'Dark Continent', and Stanley and Livingstone's historic meeting was a decade into the future. The conditions for picture taking confound belief. He laboured for hours in his wicker dark-room in the sweltering heat of the desert, while the volatile chemicals fizzed dangerously in their trays. Back in London he exhibited his photographs and was 'rapturously cheered' by members of the Royal Society. His reputation as a photographer was made overnight.

By the 1870s the railways had threaded their way across the country, and Bank Holidays and half-day Saturdays had been made obligatory by Act of Parliament. All of a sudden the working man and his family were able to enjoy days out, take holidays, and see a little more of the world.

With typical business acumen, Francis Frith foresaw that these new tourists would enjoy having souvenirs to commemorate their days out. For the next thirty years he travelled the country by train and by pony and trap, producing fine photographs of seaside resorts and beauty spots that were keenly bought by millions of Victorians. These prints were painstakingly pasted into family albums and pored over during the dark nights of winter, rekindling precious memories of summer excursions. Frith's studio was soon supplying retail shops all over the country, and by 1890 F Frith & Co had become the greatest specialist photographic publishing company in the world, with over 2,000 sales outlets, and pioneered the picture postcard.

Francis Frith had died in 1898 at his villa in Cannes, his great project still growing. By 1970 the archive he created contained over a third of a million pictures showing 7,000 British towns and villages.

Frith's legacy to us today is of immense significance and value, for the magnificent archive of evocative photographs he created provides a unique record of change in the cities, towns and villages throughout Britain over a century and more. Frith and his fellow studio photographers revisited locations many times down the years to update their views, compiling for us an enthralling and colourful pageant of British life and character.

We are fortunate that Frith was dedicated to recording the minutiae of everyday life. For it is this sheer wealth of visual data, the painstaking chronicle of changes in dress, transport, street layouts, buildings, housing and landscape that captivates us so much today, offering us a powerful link with the past and with the lives of our ancestors.

Computers have now made it possible for Frith's many thousands of images to be accessed almost instantly. The archive offers every one of us an opportunity to examine the places where we and our families have lived and worked down the years. Its images, depicting our shared past, are now bringing pleasure and enlightenment to millions around the world a century and more after his death. For further information visit: www.francisfrith.com

FRITH PRODUCTS & SERVICES

Francis Frith would doubtless be pleased to know that the pioneering publishing venture he started in 1860 still continues today. Over a hundred and forty years later, The Francis Frith Collection continues in the same innovative tradition and is now one of the foremost publishers of vintage photographs in the world. Some of the current activities include:

INTERIOR DECORATION

Today Frith's photographs can be seen framed and as giant wall murals in thousands of pubs, restaurants, hotels, banks, retail stores and other public buildings throughout the country. In every case they enhance the unique local atmosphere of the places they depict and provide reminders of gentler days in an increasingly busy and frenetic world.

PRODUCT PROMOTIONS

Frith products are used by many major companies to promote the sales of their own products or to reinforce their own history and heritage. Frith promotions have been used by Hovis bread, Courage beers, Scots Porage Oats, Colman's mustard, Cadbury's foods, Mellow Birds coffee, Dunhill pipe tobacco, Guinness, and Bulmer's Cider.

GENEALOGY AND FAMILY HISTORY

As the interest in family history and roots grows world-wide, more and more people are turning to Frith's photographs of Great Britain for images of the towns, villages and streets where their ancestors lived; and, of course, photographs of the churches and chapels where their ancestors were christened, married and buried are an essential part of every genealogy tree and family album.

FRITH PRODUCTS

All Frith photographs are available Framed or just as Mounted Prints and unmounted versions. These may be ordered from the address below. Other products available are - Calendars, Jigsaws, Canvas Prints, Mugs, Tea Towels, Tableware and local and prestige books.

THE INTERNET

Over several hundred thousand Frith photographs can be viewed and purchased on the internet through the Frith websites!

For more detailed information on Frith products, look at **www.francisfrith.com**

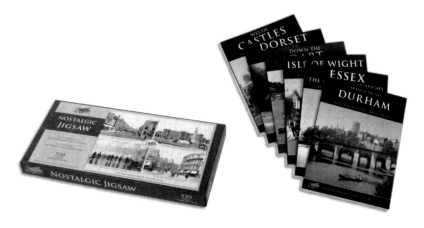 

See the complete list of Frith Books at: www.francisfrith.com
This web site is regularly updated with the latest list of publications from The Francis Frith Collection. If you wish to buy books relating to another part of the country that your local bookshop does not stock, you may purchase on-line.

For further information, trade, or author enquiries please contact us at the address below:
The Francis Frith Collection, Unit 19 Kingsmead Business Park, Gillingham, Dorset SP8 5FB.
Tel: +44 (0)1722 716 376   Email: sales@francisfrith.co.uk

See Frith products on the internet at www.francisfrith.com

FREE PRINT OF YOUR CHOICE
CHOOSE A PHOTOGRAPH FROM THIS BOOK
+ POSTAGE

Mounted Print
Overall size 14 x 11 inches (355 x 280mm)

TO RECEIVE YOUR FREE PRINT

Choose any Frith photograph in this book

Simply complete the Voucher opposite and
return it with your payment (to cover postage
and handling) and we will print the photograph
of your choice in SEPIA (size 11 x 8 inches) and
supply it in a cream mount ready to frame
(overall size 14 x 11 inches).

Order additional Mounted Prints
at HALF PRICE - £19.00 each (normally £38.00)

If you would like to order more Frith prints
from this book, possibly as gifts for friends and
family, you can buy them at half price (with no
additional postage costs).

Have your Mounted Prints framed

For an extra £20.00 per print you can have your
mounted print(s) framed in an elegant polished
wood and gilt moulding, overall size
16 x 13 inches (no additional postage required).

IMPORTANT!

❶ Please note: aerial photographs and photographs
with a reference number starting with a "Z" are not Frith
photographs and cannot be supplied under this offer.

❷ Offer valid for delivery to one UK address only.

❸ These special prices are only available if you use this
form to order. You must use the ORIGINAL VOUCHER on
this page (no copies permitted). We can only despatch
to one UK address.

❹ This offer cannot be combined with any other offer.

As a customer your name & address will be stored by Frith but not sold or rented
to third parties. Your data will be used for the purpose of this promotion only.

Send completed Voucher form to:

**The Francis Frith Collection,
19 Kingsmead Business Park, Gillingham,
Dorset SP8 5FB**

Voucher for **FREE** and Reduced Price Frith Prints

*Please do not photocopy this voucher. Only the original is valid,
so please fill it in, cut it out and return it to us with your order.*

Picture ref no	Page no	Qty	Mounted @ £19.00	Framed + £20.00	Total Cost £
		1	Free of charge*	£	£
			£19.00	£	£
			£19.00	£	£
			£19.00	£	£
			£19.00	£	£
			£19.00	£	£

*Please allow 28 days for delivery.
Offer available to one UK address only*

* Post & handling		£3.80
Total Order Cost		£

Title of this book . . . .

I enclose a cheque/postal order for £ . . . .
made payable to 'The Francis Frith Collection'

OR please debit my Mastercard / Visa / Maestro card,
details below

Card Number:

Issue No (Maestro only):   Valid from (Maestro):

Card Security Number: Expires:

Signature:

Name Mr/Mrs/Ms . . . .

Address . . . .

. . . .

. . . .

. . . . Postcode . . . .

Daytime Tel No . . . .

Email . . . .

Valid to 31/12/20

Free Print – see overleaf

Can you help us with information about any of the Frith photographs in this book?

We are gradually compiling an historical record for each of the photographs in the Frith archive. It is always fascinating to find out the names of the people shown in the pictures, as well as insights into the shops, buildings and other features depicted.

If you recognize anyone in the photographs in this book, or if you have information not already included in the author's caption, do let us know. We would love to hear from you, and will try to publish it in future books or articles.

An Invitation from The Francis Frith Collection to Share Your Memories

The 'Share Your Memories' feature of our website allows members of the public to add personal memories relating to the places featured in our photographs, or comment on others already added. Seeing a place from your past can rekindle forgotten or long held memories. Why not visit the website, find photographs of places you know well and add YOUR story for others to read and enjoy? We would love to hear from you!

www.francisfrith.com/memories

Our production team

Frith books are produced by a small dedicated team at offices near Salisbury. Most have worked with the Frith Collection for many years. All have in common one quality: they have a passion for the Frith Collection.

Frith Books and Gifts

We have a wide range of books and gifts available on our website utilising our photographic archive, many of which can be individually personalised.

www.francisfrith.com